THE RHYTHM OF LIFE

THE RHYTHM OF
LIFE

An Antidote for
Our Busy Age

MATTHEW KELLY

Beacon
PUBLISHING

Beacon Publishing is a division of The Matthew Kelly Foundation.

First Edition published 1999.

Library of Congress Cataloging-in Publication Data

Kelly, Matthew
      The rhythm of life : an antidote for our busy age /
Matthew Kelly. - first edition
      ISBN   1-929266-01-4 (cloth.)
1.Human Development.   2. Spirituality.   3. Recovery.
4. Kelly, Matthew.
I Title.

01 02 03 04 • 14 13 12 11 10 09 08 07 06 05 04

TABLE of CONTENTS

When I was a child, one of my teachers took me aside, crouched down to my level, looked deep into my eyes and said, "Let your life be guided by greatness."

Over the years, and particularly as I have written this book, I have continually called out into the deep abyss of the past to my ancestors and the people of other ages—far back to the beginning of time.

I have cried out to every brave man and woman in history who ever attempted to reach out and grasp at excellence and greatness. I have reached into the past and beckoned them, pleaded with them, and begged them to come forth into the present.

I have asked them to share with me their stories, their secrets, and their strength. They are legends, heroes, leaders, champions, and saints. Each day I reach back and try to draw the best of each of them into myself. They never resist. I dedicate this book to them. To everyone of generations past who labored to enrich, ennoble, and empower the people of their age.

I dedicate this book also to the people of the present age who are working tirelessly for the same cause, and to the people of future generations who will carry on this work.

Mostly I dedicate this book to you, that you may become one of those people.

—*Matthew Kelly*

THE RHYTHM OF LIFE

Do not let your life be like a shooting star which lights up the sky for only a brief moment.

Let your life be like the sun that always burns brightly in the heavens, bringing light and warmth to all those on earth.

CHAPTER 1

CRISIS

This book is based upon personal crisis. My own. They say a crisis brings the best out of people. They say if it doesn't kill you, it makes you a better person.

It didn't kill me.

I must confess, I am anything but comfortable writing about myself. I think I fear being perceived as prideful or self-important. In my other writings I have tried to avoid it wherever possible, but many of my friends and colleagues have often commented, "You need to give the reader more of Matthew Kelly." In this case, the only way to avoid writing about myself would be not to write—and at the same time, I feel I must write about these things. A little betwixt,

I sense that I am writing as much for myself as I am for you.

—⁓—

I grew up in Sydney, Australia, with my brothers: Mark, Simon, Andrew, Brett, Nathan, Bernard, and Hamish. Having seven brothers meant bunk beds, hand-me-down clothes, and never a dull moment. Apart from the fact that I had seven brothers, until I was nineteen I lived what I think could be described as a fairly normal life.

For nineteen years I had been floating along just fine. Throughout high school I had gathered a handful of close friends, thrived on the sporting field, dated some wonderful girls, held an afternoon job at a drug store delivering packages to the elderly, and had even grown to quite enjoy my studies. I had also fallen for the classic modern lie—life is about success, and success is the fast car, the big house, the important job, and lots of money. Believing that, I was in college studying toward a degree in marketing, preparing for my ascent to the upper realms of the corporate world. It was at this time that extraordinary things began to take place for me.

All of a sudden, I began to think about life—and death, greed, fear, love, God, society, suffering, forgiveness, history, and particularly whether or not I was put here for any real purpose. Our lives change when we stop merely replying to questions, and begin to ask them. I started asking questions.

In no time at all life started responding to my questions. And as my reflections grew deeper I noticed that I was beginning to approach everyone and everything in my life differently. I was discovering a sense of the miraculous in the everyday. It was as if I had found some coveted treasure or secret. I felt a fire within me— an intense passion for life, and at the same time, an un-shakeable peace.

On the outside little had changed. On the inside I was developing an exciting new awareness.

Later that same year, an opportunity emerged for me to give a talk to a small group of people at a home in Castle Hill, a suburb of Sydney. It wasn't something that I felt particularly comfortable with, but I had a real desire to share some of the ideas that my soul-searching had given birth to during the preceding months.

Although I was not aware of it at the time, speaking to a handful of people on October 8, 1993, was to be-come a very significant event. One that would com-pletely change the direction of my life.

The following week I found myself giving four talks, the week after that six—and it was then that life invited me down unimaginable paths.

I discovered my gift and my life changed.

Between October of 1993 and August of 1997 I gave almost seven hundred talks and seminars to audi-ences that totaled over 750,000 people in forty-one countries. I was twenty-four years old, had published four books in six languages, had a constant barrage of invitations to speak all over the world, I was appear-ing regularly on television and radio programs, and receiving more than one hundred letters a week from readers and listeners. Publishing companies were clamoring over my books, I had just received my first serious offer to do my own radio show, and was being courted by two television networks. I was constantly meeting the most extraordinary people and every opportunity was being laid before me.

It had all happened so quickly.

—*◊◊◊*—

On the outside everything seemed fine. On the inside I was deeply troubled. I wasn't a sign of contradiction, I was a walking contradiction. The authentic life I espoused to, and wrote and spoke about so passionately, had been lost somewhere along the way.

One Tuesday morning early in August of 1997 I woke at about eleven o'clock. I had slept through the alarm and was literally unable to drag myself out of bed. It was not the first time. In fact, for months I had been sleeping for ten, twelve, sometimes fourteen hours a day. I was completely exhausted.

I rolled over and slept until about four o'clock that afternoon.

When I finally did get out of bed I called the doctor, and over the next several days I went through the physical, emotional, and mental anguish of medical tests. I was then told that there was nothing wrong with me other than the fact that I was suffering from chronic levels of fatigue and exhaustion.

It had been coming for some time. I had seen it coming and ignored it. I suppose I didn't want to admit something was wrong. I was in denial.

My life was a complete mess. Nothing was right. Although I was still constantly hopping from continent to continent, I was now based in America. Everything seemed to bother me, and confusion and chaos were the only regular feelings I could express. I felt overwhelmed. Everything important to me was slipping away, and the people I loved were the very people I was disappointing and hurting. I had never felt more alone. I was miserable. I had lost my roots.

My diet was atrocious, I could count on one hand the number of times I had exercised in the past six months, and my sleeping pattern was appalling.

Physically I was exhausted. Emotionally I was confused and hurting. Intellectually I was starving. And spiritually I was as dry as the Sahara desert.

The well was empty.

My lifestyle had caught up with me. I was too young to feel this old. I had fallen victim to my own misplaced priorities. I was forced to admit that the general day-to-day structure of my life was fatally flawed.

I had lost *The Rhythm of Life.*

———ᗯᗯ———

My doctor suggested a break from speaking, writing, and traveling. He sat me down in his office and gave me a long speech explaining that he felt I should take at least three months off. "Impossible," I thought.

At the time my schedule was being booked twelve months in advance, my fourth book had just been released, and a very large fall speaking tour had long been planned.

I explained this to the doctor who told me, with no hesitation and the greatest ease, that I was a fool. "If you don't take time to recover now, you could develop problems that will last a lifetime," he said. And continued, "Matthew, you are only twenty-four, and you can go on speaking and writing for fifty years, but you need to take care of yourself. And right now, that means taking three months off."

That was a turning point in my life. A moment of salvation. In that moment, assisted by some mysterious grace, I got off the merry-go-round which was my life.

—∿∿—

Two weeks later, in the fall of 1997, I took three months away from my speaking schedule and went to Europe to study. I spent that time in what was once a monastery, in the small village of Gaming, Austria. My experience there became one of reflection, refreshment, and renewal.

In the classroom I was studying German and medieval history. Outside the classroom I was learning a lot about myself. But my exhaustion and pain continued to haunt me, and I began to wonder whether the intense passion for life that had emerged four years earlier would ever again return.

I suppose that's what makes a crisis a crisis, the fact that you don't know when it will end, what the outcome will be, or even if it will end.

As the days and weeks passed my reflections led me to take a good, long, hard look at myself, my lifestyle, and the world in which we live. It was then that I made some discoveries so important that they have changed my approach to life forever—truths I had overlooked my whole life.

The first of these discoveries was my legitimate need. It dawned on me that I am a human being—not a machine that writes books and gives talks—and that I have some basic, but legitimate needs. This is not selfish, as I had previously believed. It's life. Some of my legitimate needs are as simple as oxygen to breathe and water to drink. Others are as complex as my need to love and be loved.

Examining the various difficulties and heartaches I was experiencing led me to see that these "legitimate needs" fall into four categories—physical, emotional, intellectual, and spiritual. I also came to realize that when these needs are satisfied I am necessarily a healthier and happier person.

In this realization, I was now face to face with all the flaws in my lifestyle of the previous four years. Many of my legitimate needs had been almost completely neglected. I had fallen into a common modern trap. My life had gathered a momentum of its own. I was just being carried along. My legitimate needs had never been considered in the creation of that lifestyle. My scheduling was never done with my legitimate needs in mind. How could it be, I wasn't even consciously aware that I had legitimate needs.

Delving into my past I discovered that the times I had experienced a sense of peace, joy, and fulfillment— and still achieved and excelled—were times when I had a certain consistency and rhythm to my life. They were the times when I had been attentive to my legitimate needs—physically, emotionally, intellectually, and spiritually. At those times all the major elements of my being were working together in harmony and moving towards a common goal.

As I looked back over the four year period, I could see that gradually I had allowed the hustle and bustle of the world to distract me, to affect me, to disorient me. It had all happened so subtly that I could not even pinpoint the time when this demise had begun.

What surprised me the most was the cause of the personal crisis I was then experiencing. It was not bad things that had led me to this lonely place of brokeness—but rather good things. Good opportunities were destroying me. I always considered an invitation to speak to a group of people as something good. Objectively, of course, it was. But recalling one day when I had traveled from New Orleans to San Francisco to Cleveland in the same day, I realized that too many good opportunities can become a dangerous situation. Even when they are opportunities to do good. Especially when they are opportunities to do good.

Good opportunities are very hard to refuse. I also came to realize that just because something is good, doesn't mean it is good for you, or right for you.

For four years I had become increasingly busier doing "good things." So much so, that they had become bad for me. They had worn me down to the point of exhaustion, and my schedule provided no opportunity for me to recover. I had adopted a lifestyle that didn't make allowance for my legitimate needs. My exhaustion led to confusion, my confusion to frustration, my frustration to poor decisions, my poor decisions led to chaos, and this chaos to disappointment.

I discovered that I was going to have to learn to say "no"—even to good opportunities, even to opportunities to do good.

———

During my time in Austria, each afternoon when my classes were finished I would take a walk. Often I would go down to the store in the middle of the village to buy some chocolate. Nothing compares to European chocolate. Just beyond the boundaries of the monastery was a small park. In the middle of the park stood one very tall strong tree.

Each day I would look at this tree and notice that despite its imperfect forms and crooked branches, it had a perfection of its own.

One night there was a fierce storm. For two hours I lay awake in my bed watching the lightning flash across the sky and feeling the thunder crash. The next day when I went walking there was debris everywhere. The trees around the monastery had lost lots of leaves, huge branches had been torn from others, and some had even been uprooted and pulled to the ground. But in the middle of the park, even though it stood alone, the great tree still stood tall, virtually unaffected by the storm. It had lost some leaves, but no major limbs, and the storm certainly hadn't uprooted it.

I learned many lessons from that tree.

A tree with strong roots grows strong. A tree with strong roots bears much fruit. A tree with strong roots bears good fruit. A tree with strong roots can weather any storm. If a tree is uprooted and replanted often, it will not be able to sink its roots deep into the earth, and therefore will not grow strong or be fruitful.

All of this is true not only for a tree, but also for a person.

The tree helped me to see that my physical, emotional, intellectual, and spiritual roots were neither strong nor deep.

———~~~———

The crisis didn't last forever, and there was no complex solution to the problems I had been experiencing. Quite the opposite, it was the simple things that restored me to health.

As the days and weeks passed, I dedicated myself to becoming more and more attentive to my legitimate needs. As I did, my withered roots began to grow and I could feel them stretching out and sinking themselves into the rich, moist earth of life. I began to eat regularly, I began to sleep regularly, to exercise and pray regularly, to study regularly, and I started to make time for rest and relaxation on a regular basis.

Then one day I heard myself laugh again. Really laugh, and I don't think I had laughed like that in a long time. The restlessness and exhaustion had dissipated. The dissatisfaction and depression had lifted, and I was once again feeling peaceful, happy, energized, excited, and passionate about life.

I started waking up to an old familiar feeling and to thoughts like, "It's good to be alive." When I looked in the mirror something seemed different. People began to comment, "You are looking really great!" or, "You seem so happy these days!" The color was back in my face and the sparkle had returned to my eyes. The simplest acts began to bring me the most intense satisfaction. Life was good.

There in the mountains, a couple of hours outside of Vienna, I rediscovered *The Rhythm of Life.*

———

When I returned from Austria I noticed that the difficulties I had experienced over the previous four years were not unique to my life or situation. In fact, I discovered that only a very few people are not suffering from identical or similar lifestyle problems.

The world is full of men and women who work too much, sleep too little, hardly ever exercise, eat poorly, and are always struggling or failing to find adequate time to spend with their families. The modern mother finds herself in a perpetual hurry—rushing from work to school to daycare to baseball to hockey to ballet to the doctor to the market to the mall to church... Even college students—living a life of leisure, in the truest sense—are always complaining about how busy they are, and the stress and pressure they are under.

The world has gone and got itself in an awful rush, to whose benefit I do not know. We are too busy for our own good. We need to slow down. Our lifestyles are destroying us.

It is clear that we have bought bigger houses, better cars, more technology, designer label clothes, and generally a higher financial "standard of living." The real questions are: What has been the cost? You cannot measure the price of everything in dollars and cents. What have we lost? Have we paid a price too high?

The simple truth is, our lifestyles are not forced upon us. We create them with our choices. Our lifestyle is the result of choices we have made, based on what we perceive as our desires and priorities.

Now is an opportunity to reassess those priorities.

—◆◆◆—

As I reflect on the world in which we live, it isn't any wonder that I fell so blindly into the traps I did.

We live in a world obsessed with noise, speed, and activity. We live in an age paralyzed by greed, lust, and violence. This climate has a tendency to be seductive, and to influence us with the greatest subtlety. Often the effects are gradual, but over time they are dramatic, even devastating.

We live in the age of paradox. What are the characteristics of this age? Perhaps they would be more appropriately thought of as "symptoms." I thought the following reflection by an anonymous author would help us to answer that question, and to take a look at our lives and our world.

"We have taller buildings, but shorter tempers; wider freeways, but narrower viewpoints; we spend more, but have less; we buy more, but enjoy it less.

We have bigger houses and smaller families; more conveniences, but less time; we have more degrees, but less common sense; more knowledge, but less judgement; more experts, but more problems; more medicine, but less wellness.

We drink too much, smoke too much, spend too recklessly, laugh too little, drive too fast, get too angry too quickly, stay up too late, get up too tired, read too seldom, watch TV too much, and pray too little.

We have multiplied our possessions, but reduced our values. We talk too much, love too seldom, and lie too often. We've learned how to make a living, but not a life; we've added years to life, but not life to years. We've been all the way to the moon and back, but have trouble crossing the street to meet the new neighbor.

We've conquered outer space, but not inner space; we've done larger things, but not better things; we've cleaned up the air, but polluted the soul; we've split the atom, but not our prejudice; we write more, but learn less; plan more, but accomplish less.

We've learned to rush, but not to wait; we have higher incomes, but lower morals; more food, but less appeasement; more acquaintances, but fewer friends; more effort, but less success.

We build more computers to hold more information, to produce more copies than ever, but have less communication; we've become long on quantity, but short on quality.

These are the times of fast foods and slow digestion; tall men and short character; steep profits and shallow relationships. These are the times of world peace, but domestic warfare; more leisure and less fun; more kinds of food and less nutrition. These are the days of two incomes, but more divorce; of fancier houses, but broken homes. These are the days of quick trips, disposable diapers, throwaway morality, one-night stands, overweight bodies, and pills that do everything from cheer, to quiet, to kill.

It is a time when there is much in the show window, and nothing in the stockroom. Indeed it is all true."

—◦◦◦—

We live in a troubled time. This is an age of crisis. Not only personal, but also social and cultural crisis. It is my belief that any adequate solutions to the challenges that face us in the world today must be both accessible and applicable to everyone, everywhere, regardless of age, color, creed, or culture. Furthermore, the practicality of these solutions must impact and be deeply intertwined with people's day-to-day living.

My experience and reflection lead me to believe that one of our greatest challenges in the modern world is lifestyle. In today's hectic world we often push ourselves to the limit—sometimes forgetting that our bodies, hearts, minds, and spirits all need time to refocus and recharge. Striving for a balanced lifestyle—one which enables us to maintain a natural state—will ensure optimum health and well-being. *The Rhythm of Life* is a passport to achieving this balance.

—◆—

The Rhythm of Life is a lifestyle. It is a way of life that makes allowance for, and leads to the fulfillment of, all our legitimate needs—physically, emotionally, intellectually, and spiritually.

The Rhythm of Life is the perfect combination of rest, activity, and pace, which ennobles us to become the unique individual we were created to be, enables us to excel in all we do, and empowers us with a certain clarity of mind and peace of heart.

The Rhythm of Life is an antidote for our age.

I believe that life should be lived passionately, and I believe that the day-to-day drudgery that stifles the greatness of the human spirit should be avoided at all costs. I do not despise simple daily tasks, but I believe their place is in building us up, not in tearing us down.

As we venture into the new millennium, the challenge life presents to us all is to develop a balance between activity and thought. But particularly, to fill our lives with action which springs forth from contemplation.

Look at the world. Look at yourself. Look at your lifestyle. Ponder these things. Our chaotic world and complex lives are crying out for a little order and simplicity.

Most people stumble through life believing that one day they will find the pace of life and variety of activity that will create *The Rhythm of Life* which is conducive to optimum health, happiness, efficiency, and contentment. They will not. *The Rhythm of Life* must be desired and created.

We make a thousand lifestyle choices everyday. Those decisions either create or destroy the natural rhythm of life.

Life is not a hundred meter dash, it's a marathon.

There is more to life than increasing the speed. Faster isn't always better, bigger isn't always better, louder isn't always better. More isn't always the solution. Life is not a competition to see who can collect the most expensive toys. The best things in life are not things—and sometimes less is more.

Find *your* rhythm.

CHAPTER 2

WHAT DO YOU WANT FROM LIFE?

left the old monastery in Austria just before Christmas of 1997. Since then I have resumed my speaking and writing, but in doing so, I have dedicated myself to creating a lifestyle that lends itself to the authentic life I aspire to live. One of the questions that my crisis situation forced me to ask and answer was: What do you want from life?

⸺⸺

Not so long ago I was invited to speak to a group of seniors at a high school in Cape May on the Jersey shore. We began our discussion with a line from a song which was on the charts at the time entitled 3am, by a group called Matchbox 20—*"She believes that life is made up of all that you're used to."*

Have you ever noticed that the majority of people who are born into a high socioeconomic family spend their whole lives in that higher socioeconomic class? Similarly, have you ever noticed that people who are born into a low socioeconomic family tend to remain in that class their whole lives? The same is true of the middle class. "She believes that life is made up of all that you are used to." The things we are used to, the things we expect to happen in our lives, usually do. The great British novelist, Sommerset Maugham, once wrote, *"It's a funny thing about life, if you refuse to accept anything but the best, that is very often what you will receive."*

People who are able to pass from a lower socioeconomic class to a higher socioeconomic class fill their hearts and minds with hope, expectation, and acceptance. They form the mind-set of someone who already exists in the higher socioeconomic group. Internally they become "used to" the things that are associated with being part of that group, and over time their daily actions lead them to join that group.

The same is true of a person who passes from riches to poverty. Even amidst wealth and abundance he focuses on what is lacking, on what he does not have. It is usually people who have little or nothing, people of lower socioeconomic classes, that focus on their lack. Before long, he has filled his heart and mind with lack and poverty and internally he has become "used to" the things associated with being part of a lower socioeconomic group. Over time his daily actions lead him to join that group.

The most striking example is that of lottery winners. Studies show that seventy percent of people who win the lottery return to the same socioeconomic group within five to ten years. They simply do not know how to manage their new found financial wealth. They are not "used to" it.

The students in Cape May that day agreed that life for the most part delivers to us the things we expect and are used to. Together we concluded that it is important to get used to the things we want, the things that are good for us—and hopefully these are one and the same.

—⁓—

I then asked them how long it would be until they graduated. In a burst of excitement and energy they replied in unison "eleven days."

From there, our discussion entered into the unbounded territories of these young men and women's dreams and imaginations. There were eighty-four students before me. Representatives of the future. I was curious. I wanted to be invited into their hearts and minds. I invited myself by asking, "What do you want from life?"

For a few moments there was silence. Then realizing that my question was not rhetorical, a young man called out, "I want to be rich." I investigated with a couple of questions and discovered that this young man was hoping to join the Navy and had aspirations beyond that in commercial engineering. I asked him how much money would make him rich enough to satisfy this desire and dream he had. He didn't seem to know, so I asked him, "Do you know anyone who is thirty years old and has

$100,000 in cash which they have earned themselves?" He said that he didn't know any such person. I then asked him if he had $100,000 cash at the age of thirty, would he consider himself on his way towards being "rich." He agreed that he would be well on the way. So I assured him that the U.S. Navy would reward him sufficiently to achieve this if he was determined, and persisted in his desire and dream.

I then expounded for him a simple analysis of earning, saving, and investing that my older brother Simon laid before me when I was fifteen. "If you save $100 each week for twelve years, how much will you have?" I asked. "$62,400," he replied after some deliberation. "But if you invest that $100 per week at 7.5% compounding interest, at the end of twelve years, how much will you have?" He shrugged his shoulders. "$102,988.35," I announced.

The young man smiled and I wished him every success in his quest for monetary riches.

Then I raised the question again, "What else do you want from life?"

A young woman proclaimed her desire to be a doctor. I asked her why she wanted to be a doctor. She replied, "So that I can help people, relieve suffering, and make a lot of money."

We agreed that if she continued to work hard and remained dedicated to her studies and her dream, that she would one day become a doctor. I wished her every success and encouraged her to try to keep her motives in her heart in the same order she had stated them, "to help people, to relieve suffering, and to make a lot of money."

I then asked the question again, "What else do you want from life?"

One young man then called out, "I want a beautiful wife." I asked him if he had been successful in locating one yet. He said that he hadn't and I sympathized with him, explaining that I had not either.

I then asked him if he knew what he was looking for in a woman. He said he did. So I explained that the best way to attract that kind of person was to become that kind of person.

And so I asked the question again, "What else do you want from life?"

This time a young man with a firm and confident voice said, "The President. I want to be the President of the United States of America."

I then proceeded to ask him how he intended to achieve this goal. He unfolded for me and his fellow students a plan which included undergraduate studies in international business and political science, then law school, local political campaign involvement, a number of summer internships on Capital Hill, a time in the United States Army, and an array of community service.

It was clear that this dream had not entered his head during this brainstorming session that I had brought upon these high school seniors. His wasn't a pipe dream. The nature of this dream was not of the vain dreaming we do while we sleep, but rather of the dreaming that we do in the daylight hours, which gives birth to purposeful living and forms our future. Perhaps one day he will become the first African American President of the United States of America!

I wished him well in his endeavors. The mood had changed. The young minds before me had been dragged deeper into this dream-making session by the real- ization that one of their peers had spent a lot of time thinking about this very question. So I asked it again, "What else do you want from life?"

A young man said, "Happiness—I want to be happy." I asked him if he knew how he would find or achieve this happiness in his life, but he didn't. I asked him if he could describe it, but he couldn't. I assured him that his desire for happiness was a noble one and that we would talk about it later in our discussion. Twenty-five minutes later we returned to him and discussed how he might find that happiness—but that comes a little later in this book.

I asked the question again, "What else do you want from life?"

A young woman said, "A gorgeous man who is kind and loving." I asked her, as I had asked the young man earlier, had she succeeded in locating one yet. She wasn't shy and she volleyed by saying, "How will I know when I find him? How will I know he is the one?"

"Not because he tells you he loves you. Not because of the gifts he gives you. Not because of the way that he looks at you. And, it certainly is not 'in his kiss.'" They laughed, and I continued, "At least these things alone are not enough upon which to decide. You see, love is not what love says. Love is not what love says it will do, or even promises it will do. Love is what love does. And gifts—chocolates and flowers, jewelry and fancy clothes, these are not gifts. Often, these are only excuses and apologies for not giving the only true gift—a portion of one's self. When you are wondering, pondering, and praying to discover if he really is the one for you, consider this one idea, You deserve to be cherished. Cherished!" We held eye contact for a moment or two, her eyes began to well with tears, and I knew she understood.

Now, the room was filled with a profound silence as I asked the question again, "What do you want from life?"

After a few moments of that silence a crowd exudes when it is almost exhausted of input, a young lady said, "I want to travel."

I explained to her that in the last five years I had traveled more than a million miles, visited over forty countries, and that I hoped this qualified me to speak on the subject. "More isn't always better, sometimes it is just more. This is true in relation to most things. Travel is one of them. I think everyone should try to travel as early in their adult life as possible—and that means getting a job, working hard, and saving the money necessary. Don't go everywhere, but to a few places. Don't let your visits be too brief, nor too long, but long enough to emerge from the experience with some understanding of the lives and culture of the local people."

I continued, "Some people consider traveling to be a waste of money. Personally, I believe there is no education better than the education you get when you travel.

"Travel opens our minds to different cultures, philosophies, and world views. Travel opens our hearts to the people of foreign lands and their different traditions and creeds. Travel dissolves the stains of prejudice that infect our hearts and societies. "Money spent on travel is money well spent on an education that you will never receive from a book, or in a classroom."

I asked the question one more time, "What do you want from life?" but now the crowd was quiet, and exhausted, and still.

I was surprised. I was disappointed. I felt a deep, sharp pain within me.

In less than twenty minutes, eighty-four high school seniors had become exhausted of their dreams, ambitions, and plans for the future. If that was not completely true, then whatever they had failed to share, they felt was not worth sharing. Seven students had been able to express the dreams of all eighty-four. Was I still in the land of infinite dreams and opportunities? I wondered.

If I had asked them to tell me what was wrong with the education system our discussion might have lasted for hours. If I had asked them about their favorite sporting highlight, or television sitcom, the discussion might have lasted all day. But after all, these are things that affect them, things that they are interested in! Are the people of today more interested in spectator sports and television sitcoms than they are in their own future?

Men and women wander the earth marveling at the highest mountains, the deepest oceans, the whitest sands, the most exotic islands, the most intriguing birds of the air and fish of the sea—and all the time never stop to marvel at themselves and realize their infinite potential as human beings.

—◦◦◦—

What had begun as an impromptu question that day has become a regular part of my dialogue with young people in schools and colleges around the world. I cannot help but feel that their educational experience is not preparing them adequately to attend the rich banquet of life. Certainly they are capable of performing all types of complex problems and specific tasks, but who and what do these serve if they cannot think for themselves? If they have no understanding of the meaning and purpose of their own lives? If they do not know who they are as individuals?

Since that day in Cape May I have spent countless hours asking friends, colleagues, loved ones, and strangers on planes—"What do you want from life?" For the most part the answers have been vague and general, not thought out. Most people seem surprised by the question. I have been accused of being too deep on a number of occasions—and only on a rare occasion does someone say, "I want these things..., for these reasons..., and this is how I intend to achieve them..." Their answer we will discuss shortly. But first, at this early part of this book and this early stage of our journey together, I would like to put the same question to you: What do you want from life?

Think about it. Ponder it. Write your answers down. Make a list. Keep that piece of paper.

Put this book down now—and before you read on spend five minutes, or five hours, answering this question for yourself. If you have already thought about it long and hard and can write the answers down quickly—wonderful. If you have never taken time to seriously address this question, don't pretend that you have. Take the time. Think it over. Carefully think about what you want from life. Start a new notebook. Your answers don't have to be definitive. They will change over time. That's okay. But it is still important to write them down now. It will help you as you read through the rest of this book and as you venture through the rest of your life.

If you do not know what you want from life, everything will appear either as an obstacle or as a burden.

But history has taught us, the whole world gets out of the way for people who know what they want and where they are going. Be assured, if you don't know where you are going, you are lost.

Do not say, "I am too old." Titian painted a masterpiece at ninety-eight. Verdi was seventy-four when he wrote his great opera *Othello*, and eighty when he wrote *Falstaff*.

Whether you are sixteen or sixty, the rest of your life is ahead of you. You cannot change one moment of your past, but you can change your whole future.

THE MEANING OF LIFE

As a child I was always the one who wanted to stay at home during our school holidays, while my brothers always wanted to go away on vacations. Even during my teenage years, I remember my brothers sharing their travel dreams at the dinner table. Andrew always wanted to follow the legendary *Tour de France* through the gorgeous French alps and down into the streets of Paris. Brett wanted to ski in Italy. Greece and Israel seemed to be Nathan's pleasure, and Bernard always wanted to visit the Caribbean.

It is the source of some amusement that I, who didn't care much for travel, have been the one to travel the world. My travels have been an eye opening experience. I have been so many places, seen so many faces, and it seems I am always on my way to something new. But each place and each face makes a contribution to who I am, what I do, and how I do it.

In my travels recently I am noticing some very disturbing signs. They are trends emerging in our society that are telltale signs that all is not well in the hearts and minds of the people.

Have you noticed that fewer people are getting married these days? Have you noticed that more marriages are ending in divorce or separation? Have you noticed that youth suicide has reached epidemic levels? Have you noticed how it is much more common these days for people to change professions? Some two, three, four times? Are you noticing that more and more young people are despairing about their partner's inability, hesitancy, or unwillingness to commit? There is a crisis of commitment in our society. People seem unwilling to make commitments, or once made, unable to fulfill them.

As great as this crisis of commitment may seem, it is only secondary to a more fundamental problem. Many people sincerely try to fulfill their commitments by strengthening their minds and wills, and by employing all types of positive thinking, and yet, they are still unable to fulfill their commitments, or live up to the resolutions they make. This crisis of commitment is the result of a far more serious crisis of purpose.

People at large have lost any sense of the meaning and purpose of life. Without an understanding of our own purpose there can be no true commitment. Whether that commitment is to marriage, family, study, work, God, or relationships, it will be almost impossible to fulfill without a clear and practical understanding of our purpose. Commitment and purpose go hand in hand.

Commitment is the logical and natural response that follows from an understanding of our purpose.

—᷍ᴧᴧ᷍—

Everything in our lives is either pursued or rejected according to whether or not it will lead or assist us, and others, in the fulfillment of what we perceive as our purpose.

—᷍ᴧᴧ᷍—

Why has the occurrence of mental illness, particularly depression, elevated so dramatically in the last twenty years? Can you imagine anything more depressing than not having any sense of the meaning and purpose of your own life?

Why do so many young people get caught up in sex, drugs, alcohol, video games and loud music? They use these things to distract themselves from the frightening reality of facing a life of which they do not know the purpose and meaning.

Why do so many people get so caught up in their work that they do not have any time for anything else, even the people they love and care for? Fulfillment and achievement in their work gives them a false sense of purpose in their lives. And because they consciously, or subconsciously, believe that their work is their purpose, they completely commit to that purpose and refuse to let anything come between them and the fulfillment of what they have falsely perceived as their purpose.

Why do women so often share with me the sad situation of a husband who has no time for anything but work, no time for his children, no time for his wife? The reason is, he doesn't see his wife and children in relation to his purpose. He perceives his purpose as success and achievement in his work. The only place his wife and children have in this scheme, is that the financial fruits of his work allow him to provide for his family.

Why are people having fewer and fewer children? Children are perceived as "nice to have" if you've got the time, the money, and are prepared to suspend, and maybe even sacrifice, your career. Young couples today do not perceive the blessing of children in relation to their true purpose, but rather, in relation to their "quasi purpose" of success in the workplace and financial independence.

For the most part, people today perceive their purpose in relation to success in the workplace and financial independence. The result is what we witness before us in our world today, and what we too often allow ourselves to be a part of—a panicked frenzy of people rushing around, working too much, working too hard, working too often, in order to splash money around the economy, by paying the mortgage on the house that they really can't afford; wearing the clothes that are inordinately overpriced because they bear the name of some famed figure; driving the car that in thirty-six months they will surrender to the leasing agent for another new one; giving less and less time to the people they love and care about, and trying to ignore the things that are really important.

There must be more to life.

―――

For thousands of years men and women of every age, race, and culture have sought to understand the meaning of life. The people of our own time are no different.

Throughout history, scientists and philosophers, theologians and artists, politicians and social activists, monks and sages, and men and women from all walks of life have discussed and debated many questions in the quest to discover the meaning of life. At this juncture in time, it appears that all of humanity's searching for knowledge and answers can be arranged under five headings, each of them a question. They are five questions that humanity has been asking consciously and subconsciously ever since human life first existed.

Indeed, whether we are aware of it or not, our whole existence is a searching to answer these five questions. You and I seek the answers to these questions directly and indirectly everyday of our lives. And how we answer these questions determines the shape, form, and direction of our lives. They are:

1. Who am I?
2. Where did I come from?
3. What am I here for?
4. How do I do it?
5. Where am I going?

These are the questions around which the writings of all religious texts are centered—including the sacred writings of Israel, the Christian scriptures, and the Bhagavad-Gita. These are the questions that form the major themes in the writings of Confucius and Lao-Tze, Homer and Euripides, Sophocles and Shakespeare, Plato and Aristotle. They are the questions that testify to humanity's age-old search for the meaning and purpose of life.

With the second question, "Where did I come from?" are bound up the ideas of creation and life. With the last question, "Where am I going?" are bound up the issues of time, death, and eternity. Most religious traditions answer the second and the last question with

"God," but the ideas bound up with these questions are complex. They deserve serious study and thought in their own right.

Questions three and four, "What am I here for?" and "How do I do it?" are born from the mysteries of love, joy, misery, happiness, suffering, and especially, the never ceasing struggle we witness and experience between good and evil. Due to their practical implications, our fascination usually falls on questions three and four. But, in order to answer these questions, "What am I here for?" and "How do I do it?" it is imperative that we try as best we can to answer the first question, "Who am I?"

Strangely, this important question—"Who am I?"—does not occupy the position of prominence that it should in the history of human thought. The first question holds the key to understanding the other four questions. Ultimately, it is only by discovering and seeking to understand who we truly are, that we come to know where we came from, what we are here for, how we achieve that mission and purpose, and where we are going. The difficulty which emerges is that while we all share many characteristics in common, essentially we are each individual and unique—and so the question becomes: Who are you?

Philosophically this may all be very sound. Practically, however, the process of answering these five questions and conforming our lives to the answers we find is very difficult.

In our own place, in our own time, and in our own way we each seek to answer these questions. Experience is a wonderful, though sometimes brutal, teacher. And yet, at the same time, it is a great ignorance to believe that experience is the only teacher. As we grow wiser we realize that life is too short to learn all of her lessons from personal experience, and that, other people, places, and times have the fruit of their experiences to hand on to us.

If personal experience was the only way to learn life's lessons, these words I write would be completely wasted. I write these words to tell you the story of a time in my own life which was bitter and harsh, and to share with you the lessons I learned in the hope that you might avoid that same experience.

—∿∿—

When you were created, what do you suppose God had in mind? Were you created to do something? Were you created to have something? Were you created to be something? Were you created to become something?

The focus of our society is on doing. People who sit next to me on planes often ask me, "What do you do?" We ask young children, "What are you going to do when you grow up?" and seniors in high school, "What are you going to do in college?" and college graduates, "What are you going to do now that you have finished your studies?" The focus of our culture is task oriented. This task oriented approach to life ignores our much higher calling and purpose.

What you become is infinitely more important than what you do, or have in this lifetime. The purpose of life is to truly become the best person you can be, the person you were created to be, not in one area of your life, but in all areas of your life. In this quest alone life becomes meaningful. What you become is the result of the life you live and the habits you form along the way.

Have you ever noticed that successful people seem to be able to do everything well? This is not because of some freak chance, but because of the foundation upon which they build their lives. The foundation of their lives is a strong commitment to personal development—to struggle to become the better person they know they can be in every area of their lives—which in turn transforms their family, relationships, community, country, and world. Truly successful people have character. Part of that character is an unwavering commitment to excellence. They know the art of discipline. Successful people just have better habits than the rest. You are your habits.

Successful people are in the habit of working hard. Lazy people are in the habit of being unsuccessful.

Whether it is success in the business world, success in the spiritual life, or success on the sporting field, the principles are the same. The application of these principles to any person's life necessarily breeds character, and in turn—success, fulfillment, and happiness.

Don't be a do person, be a be person.

————

In this task oriented culture one of the real dangers is to slip into an episodic mode of living. The happenings of our day-to-day lives can become episodic, one after another, like the episodes of a soap opera. In a soap opera, there is always something happening, but nothing ever really happens. In every episode there is drama—activity takes place, words are muttered, but nothing really happens. People abusing each other, people using each other, people talking about each other, people plotting and scheming, but nothing meaningful ever happens.

Their lives are filled with superficialities and they are constantly restless and miserable. There is no theme, no thread, just another entertaining episode.

When the days and weeks of our lives become like this, we become depressed, disillusioned, and unhappy. The reason is because without direction—based on the purpose and meaning of our lives—the emptiness of our lives is overwhelming. So much so, that we go in search of all types of distractions, most of which are self-destructive. There are moments of pleasure, but they are brief in a long succession of twenty four hour days.

What we truly desire is the fulfillment, joy, and the ecstasy that comes from continually visualizing the better person we know we can be, and struggling to become that better person.

—◦◦◦—

Pablo Picasso was walking down the street in Paris one day when a woman recognized and approached him. After introducing herself and praising his work, she asked him if he would consider drawing her portrait and offered to pay him for the piece.

Picasso agreed and sat the woman down there and then on the side of the street, brought out a sketchbook, a pencil, and began to draw the woman. A small crowd of spectators gathered very quickly, but in only a handful of minutes Picasso had finished the drawing, and as he handed it to the woman he said, "That will be five thousand francs." Surprised at the price, the woman objected saying, "But Mr. Picasso it took you only a few minutes." Picasso smiled and replied, "No, my dear woman, you are mistaken, it took me a whole lifetime."

—∿∿—

The individual experiences of our lives cannot be separated from the whole. All of life's experiences thus far
have played a part in the person you are right now. The
common reaction to this statement is to recall some negative or abusive event in our past and use it as an excuse
for the person we are today. Such adoption of victim-
hood is one of the most destructive spirits at work in
the human psyche during these modern times.

The point I am really trying to make here is that we
are not a composite of everything that has ever happened to us, but rather what happens in our lives is
almost always a result of those things we habitually
think and those things we habitually do. Life is the fruit
of discipline, or not. We are our habits. For example,
you cannot separate Tiger Woods' phenomenal performance and record crushing victory at the 1997 Masters
from the other twenty years of his life prior to that
event. His practice sessions fifteen years earlier at the
age of six were as much a part of that Masters victory as
his final approach shot to the eighteenth green.

Every disciplined effort has its own multiple reward.

—∿∿—

Artistically and professionally Pablo Picasso had a profound understanding of the value of compounding effort
and experience. His professional life had theme and
thread, direction and purpose—and was held together
as one whole. His personal life lacked that wisdom.
From lover to lover he passed, from wife to wife, from
friend to friend—always moving on, eventually desert-
ing those who loved him. In the end he abandoned all

those who were close to him. Picasso's personal life was plagued by this episodic quality we discussed earlier. He was unable or unwilling to apply the truth he had discovered professionally to the other areas of his life.

Any truth we discover must not be allowed to remain isolated in one area of our lives. Rather, any truth life reveals to us must filter into every aspect of our lives, like blood to the cells of the body. Life is one.

What we *do* in the span of our lives may bring us financial reward, status, fame, power, and respect, but lasting happiness and fulfillment are the byproducts of *becoming*. In the final analysis, what you do is of little consequence. Everything important hinges on what you become. The purpose and meaning of life is inextricably connected with the personal development of each individual.

In the words of Robert Louis Stevenson, *"To be what we are, and to become what we are capable of becoming, is the only end in life."*

THE SEVEN DREAMS

In Austria I spent a lot of time questioning what I wanted from life, and how my life would be best spent. We seem to spend our lives in the service of our desires. Sometimes those desires are good and their pursuit is to our benefit. At other times, our desires are selfish and self-destructive. If there is meaning and purpose to our lives here on earth, then the highest levels of living must be linked to discovering that meaning and fulfilling that purpose. It stands to reason then that there should be a relationship between the meaning of life and our dreams.

Earlier, I asked you to stop and consider what you wanted from life, and to write those things down. As you progress through this book, I would like you to remain open to adjusting and changing, adding and eliminating some of what you had previously written.

My reflections in Austria led me to do the same exercise. This is what I came up with. These are my seven dreams. I believe the pursuit of these will lead a person to peace and happiness, to success, satisfaction, and service, to wholeness and holiness.

They are my dreams, but they are also my dreams for you.

I have a dream for you...

1.—that you have complete control over all your mental and physical faculties and that you are slave neither to food, nor drink, nor any other substance. That you have freedom—the strength of character to do what is right in each situation.

I have a dream for you...

2.—that you are able to discern the people, activities and possessions that are most important to you. And, that you are able to give each of them their time and place according to their appropriate priority.

I have a dream for you...

3.—that you have the courage, determination, firmness, and persistence to perform the tasks that you choose, decide, and resolve to perform. That you perform them with a commitment to excellence and attention to detail.

I have a dream for you...

4.—that you discover a talent which leads you to dedicate the professional aspect of your life to some occupation you can be passionate about. That you serve your neighbor, your family and your community in this occupation, and that by it, you are able to provide for your temporal needs.

I have a dream for you...

5.—that you grow in wealth in every sense of the word, that you are never in need, and that whatever your wealth is, you share it with all you can.

I have a dream for you...

6.—that you find true love. Someone you can cherish. Someone who makes you want to be a better person. A soul-mate who can challenge you and love you. A companion who can walk with you, know you, share your joy, perceive your pain and heartache, and comfort you in your disappointments.

I have a dream for you...

7.—that you discover deep and abiding interior peace. The peace and comfort that come from knowing that who you are, where you are, and what you do is essentially good; that you are contributing to the happiness of others, and that you are progressing towards becoming the better person you know you can be.

—⁓—

Perhaps you will reject the vision of life I am laying before you in this book. That's okay. But regardless of what you choose to seek from life, which rainbow you choose to chase, there will be difficult times which will put you to the test, and you will need courage and perseverance to achieve your goals and dreams.

What is it that sets men and women of great achievement apart from the rest of humanity? What do Mahatma Ghandi, Martin Luther King Jr., John F. Kennedy, Warren Buffet, Albert Einstein, John Quincy Adams, Ronald Reagan, Charlie Chaplin, Michael Jordan, Leonardo da Vinci, Beethoven, Mother Teresa and Billy Graham all have in common? What empowers them to touch and affect so many people's lives? What allows them to grasp success and reach levels of achievement that for most people are simply unfathomable?

Passion. They are passionate about what they do. Belief. They believe in what they do. Commitment. They are committed to what they do. Courage. In the face of situations where other people would lose heart, they take heart. Perseverance. Through the discouragement of failure, rejection, and criticism, they persevere and keep at it, always staying focused on their goal and dream.

Passion, belief, commitment, courage, and perseverance.

And so it will be with your life, there will be tough times—there is for everyone. There will be times of fear and trembling. There will be times of discouragement and disillusionment. Have courage, smile, keep your chin up, laugh often, be kind to yourself, stay focused, be gracious and appreciative, think happy thoughts, and carry on regardless.

—◦◦◦—

When I was twelve years old I used to sing in the school choir and often we would sing at funerals. Whether or not I knew the person who had died, funerals have always had a very deep impact on my life. On every occasion I came away determined not to waste my life, not to take life for granted.

Every now and then I like to take a walk in a cemetery. Each tombstone tells a story. Some of the people were laid to rest last year, and others last century, but I can hear all of them calling out to me in unison, sharing with me a message, *"Life is short. Do not waste your life. Live life passionately."*

Somewhere deep within you is a desire to live out the ideal I am sharing with you in these pages. Perhaps you already feel that desire stirring within you. Foster that desire. Nurture that desire. Adopt the habit of re-kindling that desire. Otherwise, your life is in danger of becoming an utter waste. You will become like "a candle in the wind," a victim of circumstance, and every time the wind stops blowing you will wish you were living these principles. But the winds of life will blow once more, changing direction and distracting you again from what is really important. You will get caught up in the episodic cycle of the modern world, and your life will bear no signs of continuity or consistency. Yes, you will achieve things, and you will have

things, but you will be restless and anxious. Many
years from now, in the dim light of your distant memory you will remember the dreams you ignored and
abandoned. You will feel a pain that cannot be eased
or consoled.

Regret over things done can be eased over time. Regret
over things left unsaid and undone is inconsolable.

———ᴧᴧᴧ———

Itzhak Perlman is one of the finest violinists of this century. A couple of years ago Mr. Perlman agreed to attend
a charity reception after one of his concerts in Vienna.
Tickets for the champagne reception were sold for the
equivalent of five hundred American dollars per guest.

At the reception while the guests mingled, Itzhak
Perlman stood in a roped off area flanked by security
guards. One by one the guests were led into the roped
off area and introduced to Mr. Perlman. As one man entered the roped off area he stretched out his hand and
shook hands with the violinist and said, "Mr. Perlman
you were phenomenal tonight. Absolutely amazing."
Perlman smiled and said nothing. The man continued,
"All my life I have had a great love of the violin, but I
have never heard anyone play the violin as brilliantly
as you did tonight." Perlman smiled again, but said
nothing, and the man continued, "You know Mr. Perlman, I would give my whole life to be able to play the
violin like you did tonight."

Perlman smiled again and said, "I have."

———ᴧᴧᴧ———

That is the difference. While some of us are sitting
around letting the sand glass of life empty, thinking

to ourselves, "I would give my whole life to be able to do that," or "I hope that happens to me one day," people like Itzhak Perlman are getting the job done. They are giving their whole lives to the magnificent and meaningful pursuit of their dreams.

I have noticed that all men and women have dreams. I have noticed that for some people their dreams "come true" and for others they do not. Why is this? Does God have favorites? I don't think so. The reason is that some people dream and wait for their dreams to come true. Theirs is a vain type of dreaming. They look at others who they consider fortunate or lucky and think to themselves, "I hope that happens to me one day." Other people listen to the movements of their hearts, and dream their dreams based upon what they hear. Then, with a commitment to excellence, and armed with their dreams as a blueprint for their lives, they go out onto the stage of life chasing their rainbow, living life passionately, and aided by a mysterious and miraculous power, which I can only describe as the grace of God, they make their dreams come true.

—◦◦◦—

Life is too short to be lived half-heartedly, and far too short to lose ourselves in the day-to-day drudgery of the hustle and bustle. Dedicate yourself to the things that deserve your dedication.

Life is short, and you are dead an awful long time. Live life passionately.

CHAPTER 3

WHO ARE YOU?

In the late 1960's there was a young man who had a dream of becoming a famous musician. He knew exactly what he wanted, so he left high school and began to play his music wherever people would listen. But as a high school drop out and with little experience he found it very difficult to get work as a musician.

Before too long he found himself playing in small, dirty clubs and bars. Sharing his gift with drunks night after night became a discouraging habit. This was not his dream. He had dreamed of playing to sellout shows across America and around the world. He had dreamed of seeing his name in lights, of walking down the street and being stopped for autographs, of having his albums in every music store. He even dreamt one day he would play to a packed baseball stadium—an absurd thought in the late 1960's.

He had stumbled upon difficult times. Financially he was broke, professionally he was failing, and his only joy in life was the support of his girlfriend. They had so little money that they would sleep in laundromats to save the expense of a hotel. But one day, she got sick of constantly being on the road. This gypsy lifestyle was not her dream either. She had dreamt of being married to a famous musician, but had forgotten the hard work it takes to get to the top. It was not the life she had imagined, so she left him.

With his only joy in life gone he decided to commit suicide. That night the young musician made a half-hearted attempt at ending his life by drinking a bottle of furniture polish. The next day, very sick, he checked himself into a mental institution.

Less than three weeks later he checked himself out. He was a new man. He was refreshed, enthusiastic, and excited about life. He was cured. They had not given him any medication, and nor was it anything the doctors or nurses had said to him. The other patients had cured him. They reminded him of how fortunate and gifted he was, and they had shown him how much more life could be. He was given a new perspective on life.

That day, that same young man left the mental institution absolutely resolved to pursue his dream to become a famed musician. He was determined to travel and work, and do whatever was necessary to achieve his dream. Three years later he wrote a song called *Piano Man*, and today Billy Joel is known to just about every person on the planet. And yes, on June 22 and 23 in

1990, Billy Joel played to sellout crowds of 90,000 people at Yankee Stadium.

We all need a startling new perspective at least once in our lives. My experience in Austria gave me that new perspective. Billy Joel's experience in the mental institution gave him that new perspective. It is my hope that this book will give you that new perspective too.

—◁◁◁—

I have always had a real passion for music, and I have always enjoyed Billy Joel's music. On a number of occasions I have had the opportunity to see him perform live and have never found that experience to be anything less than inspiring. It is rare to find musical genius mixed with such poetic thoughtfulness.

My favorite lyric of his is from a song entitled *Scenes from Italian Restaurants*. The song tells the story of Brenda and Eddie, two high school students who were the envy of all their peers. They were that popular couple, that couple who looked and seemed perfect together. The song begins, "Brenda and Eddie were the popular steadies and the king and queen of the prom. Riding around with the car top down and the radio on. Nobody looked any finer, or was more of a hit at the parkway diner," and then Billy drops my favorite line which says so much about adolescence. With it he also defines the major barrier that prevents us from achieving greater things in, and with, our lives, *"and we never knew we could want more than that out of life."*

There is more.

In all of our lives there is a great danger to believe that who we are, where we are, and what we have, is all that there is.

There is more. Do you know what it is like to walk through the streets of Paris in the pouring rain without a worry in the world, enjoying every last drop of rain that falls on your face? Do you know what it is like to see *The Nutcracker* performed at the Sydney Opera House and sit so close that you can see the beads of sweat on the dancers foreheads? Do you know what it is like to dance with no music on a beach on the island of Crete with someone you love more than you ever imagined you could love? Do you know what it is like to feel so guided that it is as though God has his very hand on your shoulder and is whispering in your ear? Do you know what it is like to stand in the Sistine Chapel and look up in awe at Michelangelo's greatest work, listening to those around you speak in fifteen different languages, breathing more deeply than you ever have, and smelling the musty air of one of the most renowned places of worship and artistic treasure in the world? Do you know... there is more?

You cannot live without dreams. Dreams foster hope, and hope is one of the forces by which men and women live.

To dream is the easiest thing in the world. There are no limitations to dreaming. But as we grow, and experience pain, failure, criticism, and disappointment, we gradually limit our dreams. We seek to live in the comfort zone. No such thing exists. It is more difficult to live in that comfort zone than it is to follow our dreams, because the comfort zone is only an illusion, but our dreams are real.

Will you spend the rest of your life chasing an illusion or following your dreams?

I will never forget a question I once heard Dr. Robert Schuller pose in an interview with Larry King. They were discussing the effects of fear of failure on our decision process, and Schuller offered this question as a guide: *"What would you attempt if you knew you could not fail?"*

Do not be afraid to dream. Perhaps your fear is of failure. There is no shame in trying to attempt mighty things and failing. The shame is in failing to attempt those things. Michelangelo, the great Renaissance artist and poet knew the value, power, and need for dreams when he wrote, *"The greater danger for most of us is not that our aim is too high and we miss it, but that it is too low and we reach it."*

Our dreams are a self-revelation. Tell me what your dreams are and I will tell you what type of person you are. Define your dreams clearly and precisely and you will know for yourself what type of person you are. If you do not like what you discover, remember, you created your dreams, and in as much, you formed the person you are today. You can therefore recreate your dreams and become a new creation.

In Chapter Two we asked the question, "What do you want from life?" and then discussed *The Seven Dreams*. In this chapter, you will meet three friends—need, desire, and talent. If you listen to them carefully, together they will teach you how to dream and for what to dream.

The secret of life is to discover who you truly are as an individual. The art of living is to be that person. Throughout this chapter, in a hundred different ways, we are seeking to know and understand who we are individually and uniquely. Let us begin by exploring our most dominant common quality as human beings—need.

UNVEILING OUR LEGITIMATE NEEDS

My first college experience was as a marketing major in Australia. I will never forget my first lecture, it remains indelibly engraved upon my memory. The professor walked into the auditorium, laid some papers on the podium and began, "Marketing is about creating needs in consumers. It's about making people feel they need things they really don't. It's about creating a desire in people which in turn, makes them feel they need your product or service." He put it in such crude terms with a straight face. But worse than that, the people around me didn't even seem to bat an eye-lid. I was stunned. I was amazed. I looked around the lecture hall, which held six hundred people and was full beyond capacity. Everyone was writing down what he had just said—drinking from the well of wisdom before them.

My father had always taught me that the secret to good and prosperous business was to provide goods or services that satisfied a real and repetitive human need. With all their psycho-babble, seduction, and deceit, the modern marketing executive has done a marvelous job of redefining and confusing people regarding this concept of "need." We may need shoes, but we do not need a particular brand of shoes. We do of course have legitimate needs, but if we associate our needs predominantly with consumer goods, we are perhaps in greater need than ever before.

Our needs exist at many different levels. There are some things we "need" to survive, just to sustain life within us. There is a further group of needs that when satisfied, allow us to achieve and maintain optimum health and well-being. It seems we attend to the former—

those things we need to sustain our existence—because we must. But often we ignore and put off the latter—those things necessary for the health of the whole person—because we are too busy, too lazy, or they are inconvenient. In doing so we neglect the most important aspect of life—our own development and well-being.

We all have legitimate needs. The fulfillment of these needs is necessary to maintain health of body, heart, mind, and spirit. This health of the whole being restores maximum efficiency. *The Rhythm of Life* helps us to identify and fulfill our legitimate needs. Throughout this book we will discuss these needs as they fall into four categories: physical needs, emotional needs, intellectual needs, and spiritual needs.

Physical Need

Our legitimate need is most basically understood in relation to our physical well-being. If you do not eat and drink, you will die. Maybe not today, or tomorrow, but somewhere along the line you will die as a direct result of not eating and drinking.

We have a legitimate need for both food and drink. Without the satisfaction of this legitimate need our well-being is in danger, and we are reduced to a state which is less than optimum. If this legitimate need is not fulfilled, our capacity in all other areas of our life is reduced.

Emotional Need

In the emotional realm it is much more difficult to pinpoint an exact need, because if you do not fulfill your emotional needs, you will not die as a direct result of emotional starvation. However, just as if you do not eat you will get stomach cramps, so too, if we starve ourselves emotionally, certain signs will emerge. For some of us emotional starvation can lead to radical mood swings, for others a general lethargy, for others yet, anger, bitterness, and resentment. The heart suffers and the body cries out.

Emotional starvation leads to distortions in our character.

—~~~—

In Austria I quickly realized this was one area that I had severely neglected. Over the previous four years I had isolated myself. My friends from childhood and high school were in Australia, ten thousand miles away from my new life which mostly kept me in the northern hemisphere. As was my family. And as sad as it may sound, I never knew what people's motives were for befriending me in this new time of my life. That insecurity was born out of bitter experience. Besides, I was rarely in a city for more than a day, which isn't the most conducive lifestyle for forming or maintaining friendships.

There were more than a hundred American students at the school in Austria enjoying what they called their "European Experience" which lasted one semester. Every weekend, as soon as classes were over they would go— to Poland, Italy, France, Belgium, Holland, Germany, and to any number of other destinations in Europe. They would travel all night on trains for barely a glimpse of these great European countries. As the weekend drew near you could sense their passion for travel surging.

Most of the American students went to Austria just for this opportunity to travel. The studies were a means to an end. It seemed strange. I had gone there to escape travel. I had no interest whatsoever in traveling. I was happier than I had been in a long time just staying around the old monastery on weekends. Though, on occasion, I would go into Vienna on a Saturday.

But a couple of weeks into the semester, a friend I had met two years earlier asked me if I would like to join him on a trip to Switzerland. Stuart was from Canada, with a unique sense of humor and an enormous appetite and propensity for fun. I hesitated at his invitation. Not because of him, but because I had loosely resolved that I wouldn't travel during these three months. He pressed saying, "Come on. We'll have a great time, we can stay with some friends of mine, it will just be you and me, and we'll be back by Sunday night." I relented. It was one of the best decisions of my life.

When classes were over we hitched a ride to the local train station and went into Vienna. From there we took the overnight train to Geneva. We just talked, told stories, ate some bread and cheese, and traded songs on our walkmans. The next day we had lunch on the lake, wandered through the old city of Geneva, and then dined with his friend Alex and her family.

It was the strangest sensation—acceptance free of expectation. I felt like any normal twenty-four year old discovering Europe. I had been to Europe more than thirty-five times, but never like this. For forty-eight hours I was completely intoxicated with normality. It was refreshing. Exhilarating. Comforting.

My relationship with Stuart rose to a completely new level and he taught me again the great value of friendship.

That weekend I learned that "no man is an island unto himself." We are social beings—and relationship brings out the best in us.

———

For most people, their legitimate emotional needs include spending time with family, friends, a spouse, a spiritual director, a boyfriend or girlfriend.

By spending time with these people we develop a connection with the human family. In turn, these relationships allow us to experience at some level the acceptance God extends to us. These relationships also challenge us to grow, and therefore provide fulfillment and satisfaction for a number of our other emotional needs.

When I was sixteen years old I had a friend back home in Sydney who would sometimes call me and say, "Let's waste some time together one day this week." It was his line. We would go out and have coffee or dinner. We would just talk, and laugh, and share stories. Perhaps even share a passage from a book one of us was reading. It was anything but a waste of time.

In our busy world there is a tendency for us to try to box our relationships off in our schedules. Often they don't fit. That is perhaps why so many relationships fall apart in our modern society. That is perhaps why so many people "fall apart" in modern society. Relationships are not just about quality time, they are about quantity time. People who have good relationships know how to waste time together.

You cannot schedule time with your children, and you cannot schedule time with your spouse. Relationships do not thrive under the pressures of our modern day schedules. All of life's important relationships thrive under the conditions of carefree timelessness. We need to develop an awareness of our legitimate emotional needs and start to give some level of priority to personal relationships.

In order to discover *The Rhythm of Life* we need to slow down. We need to set aside the hustle and bustle of work related activities and gift our relationships with some of that carefree timelessness.

Learn to waste time with the people you love.

Intellectual Need

In the area of intellectual need, it is once again very difficult to pinpoint exactly what our legitimate needs are. Nonetheless, certain signs emerge as a result of intellectual neglect.

Each of us has been gifted with an intellect—the capacity to think, decide, reason, imagine, and dream. What we think about has a tremendous influence on the reality of our lives. We will discuss this in more detail in Chapter Six.

We all have intellectual needs. Many people are involved in intellectually engaging occupations, and yet even for these, there is a need for other types of intellectual stimulation.

Our professional intellectual efforts do not necessarily suit our own individual needs at that time, position, and place in life's journey. That is why it is so important to make time for intellectual stimulation outside of the workplace. We each need to find a balance between work-related intellectual stimulation and personal intellectual stimulation.

In this category of personal intellectual stimulation we could read magazines about fashion, gardening, sports, finance, music, or any other area of interest. We will be entertained, but it is unlikely that we will be intellectually stimulated and challenged.

To really stretch the intellect and to increase the capacities of the mind, each of us must delve into the wisdom writings. Our selections could include: the scriptures, a variety of philosophical texts, and the writings of countless spiritual leaders past and present. It is in these writings that the intellect comes face to face with the most profound questions and truths about the world, creation, God, humanity, and ourselves. These writings constantly hold before us the better person we know we can be. The wisdom writings subtly call us out of our comfort zones and challenge us to improve, develop, grow, and to live life to the fullest.

We should not allow our need for intellectual stimulation to starve by merely feeding it with work related matter, nor entertaining matter alone. Rather, we must realize that our desire for intellectual stimulation is most completely met and satisfied by wisdom writings—writings which challenge us to ponder the deeper questions, truths, and mysteries of our existence. As Mark Twain wrote, *"The man who does not read good books has no advantage over the man who cannot read them."*

The brain is an organ and like our muscles it must be exercised, or it will shrivel up and waste away. Have you ever visited a person who has been in bed for a long period of time with an illness? Their body after only a couple of months begins to atrophy. Within weeks their muscles lose their firmness and they become frightfully fragile.

—◦◦◦—

When we exercise our intellect we experience a vitality and excitement for life. Just as when we are emotionally fulfilled, we seem to be walking on sunshine. Much like when we exercise physically, we feel fresh and more fully alive. When we pray and reflect we find direction, focus, and peace.

Life is meant to be a rich and rewarding experience. Life is supposed to be full of wonder and moments of inspiration. Life is an expression of abundance and should be lived passionately. It has been my experience that our acknowledgment of these legitimate needs and our attentiveness to them brings about the opportunity to embrace life "to the fullest."

Spiritual Need

It is in the area of spirituality that we come to understand most fully our other legitimate needs—physical, emotional, and intellectual—and gain the insight to live a life that enriches, upholds, and protects our well-being in each of these areas.

Our spiritual needs are the most difficult to define. As in all areas of legitimate need, our spiritual needs often change as we move into different phases of our own personal spiritual journey. All that as it may be, there are two basic spiritual needs that are unchanging and common to us all—silence and solitude.

We all have a need to search our hearts for answers to the questions posed by our life experiences and to discover our truest desires. It has been my experience that these exercises are most effectively performed alone in the precious solitude of the classroom of silence.

It is also in silence and solitude that life's preeminent challenge is proposed to us. Silence and solitude unveil who we are with all our faults, failings, flaws, defects, talents, abilities, and potential. Brother Silence and Sister Solitude always reveal the better person we know we can be. The revelation of this dual reality—ourselves as we are now, and the better person we can become—challenges us to change and to grow. Commitment to that purpose of becoming *the better person we know we can be* is alone the key to meaningful living and to a life lived passionately. Many of life's great lessons can only be learned in the classroom of silence.

These are not new ideas. Pythagoras, the Greek philosopher and mathematician who lived from 580 B.C—500 B.C wrote, *"Learn to be silent. Let your quiet mind listen and absorb."* Blaise Pascal, the French philosopher, scientist, mathematician, and writer who lived in the seventeenth century wrote this about the importance and value of silence and solitude, *"All of man's miseries derive from not being able to sit quietly in a room alone."*

Learn to be quiet. Learn to be still.

When we attend to our legitimate spiritual needs everything else seems to fall into perspective—we are able to let go of the past, patiently wait for the future, and live with an intense passion for life in the joy of the here and now. We feel healthy. We feel alive. Our lives are filled with vitality and life becomes exciting instead of the day in, day out, drudgery of counting the minutes away. This is because we have direction in our lives. With this focus, perspective, and vitality we learn to implement the infinitely valuable wisdom of turning each and every experience of our lives into something that enriches and develops us.

Spirituality brings clarity, direction, and continuity to our lives.

———*ᴧᴧ*———

We all have needs. We need air to breathe, water to drink, and food to eat. We need to love and be loved. We need to accept and appreciate others, and to be accepted and appreciated by others. We need to learn and to grow. We need. This is our common bond as human beings. We are not as strong as we think we are. We are fragile. We are not as independent as we pretend to be. We are one in our need.

Our acknowledgement of our needs, and attentiveness to them, is the foundation upon which we will gradually develop optimum health and well-being. When we acknowledge our needs and base our lifestyle decisions on them we necessarily live healthier and happier lives.

Knowing your own legitimate needs is a major step towards knowing who you are.

THE RELATIONSHIP BETWEEN NEED AND DESIRE

For thousands of years in myths, legends, stories, fairy-tales, and parables, the heart has been defined as the place from which our desires emerge, the place where our feelings reside. Our hearts are as individual and unique as our fingerprints. I cannot presume to know or understand the movements of your heart. Nor you mine, but each of us must seek to discover and know the movements of our own hearts.

It is time now to turn the focus of our discussion from our needs to our desires. I believe that our needs and desires are divinely and providentially linked.

As human beings we were created with the desire and the capacity for good. The good we desire is the deepest desire of our hearts. These desires we should follow regardless of the cost or sacrifice involved. Our fulfillment and happiness, our wholeness and holiness, depend upon living out of the deepest desires of our hearts.

Our deepest desires are directly linked to our legitimate needs. The careful pairing of our deepest desires and legitimate needs leads to the fulfillment of all of our needs; physically, emotionally, intellectually, and spiritually. The result is a life of balance and harmony, peace and prosperity.

Physical Desire

What we truly "need" we desire, but not at the shallow levels of our hearts.

For example, you may desire six double chocolate donuts for lunch today. It is a desire, but a shallow one. At a deeper level you desire to be healthy and physically fit. The first desire for the six donuts arises in response to your legitimate need for food. But the best way to respond to that legitimate need for physical sustenance is not by devouring half a dozen donuts, but rather by enjoying a healthy, balanced, and satisfying meal.

The deeper desire of the heart—the desire to be healthy and physically fit—takes into account the whole person and views the situation from the broadest perspective.

Emotional Desire

Similar situations arise with regards to our emotional needs and desires. A common example is our desire to share certain experiences of our lives with others. Our need is to be accepted and loved.

Everyone has a bad day sometimes. This is one situation when most people need and desire to share the happenings of their day with someone else. But who we share ourselves and our experiences with is of paramount importance. You may share them with an uncooperative sales clerk, or employee by saying, "You know, I have had a really lousy day and I don't need you to treat me in that way." You will fulfill your desire to express your feelings, but your need to be loved, accepted, and understood will go on unfulfilled. Your desire to express your feelings is only a shallow representative of your deeper need to be loved, accepted, and understood.

Similarly, if you are a mother and wife and you've had a terrible day, you may be tempted to say to your misbehaving children, "Listen kids, I've had a terrible day today and I don't need you to be misbehaving." You will have fulfilled your desire to express how you feel, but the deeper need that this desire represents will remain unfulfilled.

In time we come to understand that when we feel a need to express ourselves, it is critical that we choose the right person. The sales clerk or employee doesn't know you sufficiently, and the children are too young to respond appropriately.

The fact that you had a lousy day may be a small issue for you, but the bigger the issue, the more important it is for us to express ourselves to the right person. If we open ourselves to the wrong person about the things that occupy our hearts, it is unlikely the person will reverence and respect our feelings in the way necessary. The most likely outcome of such an encounter is that we come away not feeling supported and comforted, but rather frustrated and violated.

We all have a need for a "trust relationship." A relationship with a person who will respect our feelings and reverence our struggle with the circumstances of our lives. A person who will listen and speak about these matters briefly, precisely, and with compassion, encouragement, and honesty. For some people this person is a spouse, for others it is a spiritual guide. For others this person is God and their emotional desire in this area is met through their spiritual practices. For most people it is a mixture of both their relationship with God and one or two special human friendships.

In the earlier stages of our lives we may pass through many of these relationships—classmates, members of our sporting teams, relatives, a family doctor, an older family friend, girlfriends and boyfriends, teachers, a priest or pastor. Of course, these people will not always be there when we need to express how we feel.

Experience has taught me that we can both express ourselves too much and express ourselves too little. Our first response should be to take our situation and feelings to the classroom of silence. Our restlessness and worries can often be eased by simply expressing how we feel to God.

One of our other emotional desires is to be on the other end of that trust relationship. To be the person who respects the feelings of others and has reverence for others in their struggle with the particular circumstances of their lives. Emotionally we desire to be a person who listens and a friend who can speak briefly, precisely, honestly, and yet always with encouragement and compassion.

Our emotional needs and desires are obviously vast and varied, but these principles apply in each unique case. Our needs and desires are complementary at the deepest levels.

Intellectual Desire

We are born with intellectual desire. Somewhere along the way we may have lost, distorted, or buried it because of a childhood experience or some type of conditioning. But intellectual desire is natural and abundant in us all.

The easiest way to illustrate this is with the example of a child. What do children ask? They ask, "Why?" Children are naturally curious, eager to understand, eager for knowledge.

Perhaps when you asked a question as a child you were yelled at by your parents and the shock buried that natural desire. Maybe in school as a child you asked a question in class, all the other children laughed, and the embarrassment buried that natural desire. Life doesn't spare any of us from these and other bitter—sometimes brutal—experiences. Still, we have to get back up and move on. In this case, that means redis-covering our intellectual desires.

Spiritual Desire

Our journey through the deeper levels of desire finally brings us to our spiritual desires. They lay hidden from superficiality and frivolity in the deepest recesses of the human heart. Spiritual desires are the subtlest of all, and yet they reveal the greatest of our legitimate needs. To perceive and respond to our spiritual desires is the most essential aspect of personal development

The yearnings of the senses call out for us to be at-tentive to our shallower needs and desires, but our spir-itual desires lay at the bottom of the deep, still, waters of our being.

The deepest desire of our heart is not to do something, nor to have something, but rather for peace. To simply be at peace. A deep inner peace. We all long for the peace and comfort of knowing that who we are, where we are, and what we do is essentially good, that we are contributing to the happiness of others, and that we are progressing towards becoming the better person that we know we can be. This is the prescription for peace.

The need that corresponds with that desire for peace is solitude. As we discussed earlier, and will discuss again in more detail in Chapter Five, we all have a need for solitude. To be alone. Not necessarily for long peri-ods of time, but certainly for a few minutes each day.

Do you ever feel like just going for a walk on your own? Or going to a movie on your own? Or going shopping on your own? Each of these desires are a re-sponse to a legitimate need. If we respond to our need

for solitude by going shopping alone, our need for solitude may be partially satisfied, but the distractions of
music, other people, and the host of desires that will
arise from "the mall experience" will prevent us from
drinking our fill of peace from the deep well of solitude.

In order to achieve the soul-searching that we desire
and legitimately need, it is important to find a quiet
place to be alone. In that silence and solitude we are
able to delve into the depths of our hearts.

———

To ignore our needs and desires, and their relationship
to each other, is to ignore our very selves. If you can
come to understand your needs and desires—and their
associated ambitions and motives—you will develop
amazing insights into your "self."

It would be wrong to speak of desire and not to
mention pleasure. Pleasure is at once the most wonderful and diabolical component of the human experience. Wonderful, because it is what we are created
for. Diabolical, because in the wrong form it has the
ability to keep us forever from pleasures unimagin-
ably greater.

Physical pleasure is a wonderful thing. Emotional
pleasure is something many times greater. Intellectual
pleasure is a mountain top experience in its own right.
Any situation that combines more than one of these
pleasures is an ecstasy of types. But, you have not
experienced pleasure in its purest form until you have
experienced spiritual pleasure. Peace—pure and simple—is the greatest pleasure. It is complete.

In Austria I very quickly discovered that I didn't
want the lifestyle that had kidnapped me and drained

me of my health and passion for life. Rather, I have a deep desire to be healthy in every sense of the word. My desire for food, exercise, sleep, relationship, study, and prayer were all in response to my legitimate need for these things. My deepest desires lead me to the satisfaction of my legitimate needs, which produces health and harmony within me.

Our desires and needs are very closely linked. We desire because we need. The careful matching of our deepest desires and our legitimate needs requires and demands very careful discernment. Your happiness and health depend almost entirely on the development of this ability to discern the careful matching of your legitimate needs with your deepest desires.

There is a profound and providential relationship between our needs and our desires.

THE BETTER PERSON YOU KNOW YOU CAN BE

One of the characteristics of our age is an excess of experts. Everyone is an expert it seems. We are constantly bombarded with opinions from these experts, and these opinions have a way of weaving their way into our lives and philosophies.

One example is the way news and current affair shows have a habit of presenting experts to discredit your favorite foods, normally because of the way they are manufactured. The problem with this flow of expert information is that it is presented in a rapid staccato form and never followed up. If two weeks later the expert is proven to be blatantly wrong, you will not hear a word about it. This is just one of the ways expert information is impacting our lives. All the time these expert opinions, consciously or subconsciously, are affecting the lives of millions of people. Their opinions affect our decisions.

When I was a child I never wondered what was the right or the wrong thing to do. I just knew. Something within me told me. It seems that most people can relate similarly. As children we know deep within ourselves how we should act in certain situations. We call that gentle voice within us our "conscience."

There is a lot to be said for a clear conscience. The idea doesn't get much air-time these days, but there is a tremendous tranquility born from knowing that you are doing the right thing for the right reasons.

As we grow older we seem to lose this gift of knowing which is the better way to act. Somewhere along the way most of us seem to be conditioned to distrust ourselves. We stop listening to the voice of conscience and begin to seek out the opinions of sages, seers, preachers, and experts. As a result, one of the real dilemmas that people face around the world everyday is the inability to look at a given situation and decide which is the best way to act.

Most people when faced with a financial decision consult a parent, friend, colleague, or book. Most people when faced with a personal or moral decision consult their spouse, pastor, priest, minister, friends, or the scriptures. In all of these, however, there is no constant. Different opinions and different interpretations leave many people more bewildered than they were to begin with. Finally, after gathering as much information as is available, or as much as we choose to accept, we are forced to make a decision and to act.

Between this gathering of information and our actions another process takes place: the process of decision. Decisions cannot be made in a vacuum; they are made in space and time. In order to make an effective decision, we must have some goal towards which we are moving. If not, we find ourselves deciding because, "Uncle Frank said it was the right thing to do," or "Rev. George told me it was best this way." In some cases these advisors may very well be right, but in others they may not. Regardless, we must seek to understand not only what is right, wrong, good, or best—but *why* something is right or wrong. It is also critical that we understand the effects and consequences of our actions. Not easy questions. How is the common person to know? Upon what criteria are we to base the decisions and actions of our lives?

Before we make a decision, particularly a large one, and before we give advice to assist someone else in making a decision, it is wise to take time to enter into the classroom of silence and reflect on the matter at hand. Alone in silence we discover the world, ourselves, and certain situations with greater clarity and from different perspectives. And yet, this thoughtful reflection also cannot take place in a vacuum. It must take place within the sphere of our aims, hopes, goals and dreams.

If you do not know where you are going you will never get there.

It is clear to see that the discernment of any question or opportunity in our lives depends on our understanding of where we are and where we want to go, and of who we are and who we wish to become. This brings us to one of the greatest problems the people of these times are experiencing. Most people do not know what they want. This is a tremendous disability. It makes one susceptible to becoming a pawn in other people's schemes.

No one can make you want for the right things. Nobody can make you want for anything. Desire is the fruit of a reflective heart, mind, and spirit.

—◦∿◦—

In almost every moment of the day I find I am being confronted with opportunities and questions which often seem small and insignificant, but in truth can significantly impact my lifestyle. We have options. I could watch television for an hour everyday or exercise for an hour everyday. I could eat McDonalds everyday for lunch or I can have soup and a salad. We choose between various options a hundred times a day and our choices impact our health and overall well-being.

In his classic poem, *The Road Not Taken*, Robert Frost describes coming to a fork in the road and having to choose between the two paths that lay before him. The poem does not describe one moment in a person's life, but rather, every moment. We find ourselves constantly at a crossroad. No sooner do we make one decision than another fork appears in the road.

Direction comes from a sense of purpose, and that sense of purpose helps make these daily decisions easier. I would like to share with you a model which, when properly understood, serves to discern and answer all of our questions in any area of our lives. Life can never be reduced to, or confined to, a model. But, I believe this model makes allowance for, and can be adapted to, the individual person and a particular situation, without reducing morality to a democracy, or a seemingly subjective matter.

I set this model before you now as a point of reference for discerning questions, decisions, and opportunities in our lives. More than this, it bridges the gap between knowledge of acts which are right and wrong, and the much superior knowledge of why a certain action is right, wrong, good, or best. It has become a powerful practical tool in my journey.

—–∿∿–—

The diagram below represents what is understood in the Christian tradition as the path of salvation, or the journey of the soul. Presently, we all find ourselves at *Point A*. *Point A* represents you, or me, or any individual person right now—here and today—with all of our faults, failings, flaws, defects, virtues, vices, talents, abilities, and potential.

**THE PERSON
YOU ARE NOW**

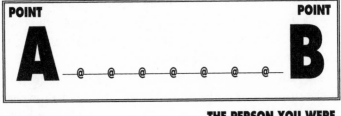

**THE PERSON YOU WERE
CREATED TO BE**

Point B represents you, or me, or any individual, as the person you were created to be—perfectly. If you close your eyes for a few moments, can you imagine ways in which you can be a better person? All of us can with relative ease. It is a simple exercise in visualization. A simple but powerful example of engaging the imagination for a good purpose.

At every point along the path closer to *Point B* we more fully recognize, appreciate, and utilize our talents and abilities, and are more dedicated to our development—physically, emotionally, intellectually, and spiritually. At each point along the path toward *Point B* there is a more harmonious relationship between our needs, desires, and talents. Through this process of transformation we begin to reach our once hidden potential. At *Point B* through the dual process of self-discovery and discovery of God, we have overcome our fears and transformed our faults and failings into virtue.

Are you dedicated to your development physically, emotionally, intellectually, and spiritually?

—*ᴧᴧᴧ*—

At *Point B* you have allowed the Divine Spirit to emerge from within. At *Point B* you allow the Divine Spirit to guide you in all your actions. At *Point B* you have reached perfection, not in a robotic sense, but in the sense that you have become perfectly the person you were created to be. By means of the journey, you have aligned your spirit with the Divine Spirit in everything, which brings you tremendous peace, happiness, and fulfillment.

All of this makes you "whole" once again. Here is the essence of the ancient term holiness—every element of your being is working together in balance and harmony. Here, the power of the four fundamental aspects of the human being—physical, emotional, intellectual, and spiritual—have all been harnessed and are being used to lead you toward perfection.

At every point along the path there is a more intimate relationship between our needs, desires, and talents. Every major world religion holds that the meaning and purpose of our lives as human beings is to give glory to God. The Egyptian monk Athanasius wrote, *"The glory of God is the perfection of the creature."* Dedicate yourself to your development—physically, emotionally, intellectually, and spiritually. This journey reveals the meaning and purpose of life.

At *Point B* you are fully aware of all your legitimate physical, emotional, intellectual, and spiritual needs. At *Point B* you have perfected the art of meeting these needs through the daily events of your life. At *Point B* you have no interest in anything that does not help you maintain that peace, balance, and harmony of life.

—⁓—

As far as I am concerned there is only one question: Will it make you a better person? If the answer to that question is "yes," do it without hesitation.

Difficulties often arise and a haze descends on our decision process when we must decide between two good opportunities. For example, a young woman is torn between becoming a doctor and a lawyer. Objectively there is no wrong in choosing and pursuing either. In reality, however, the question affects a real living person with feelings, dreams, preferences, talents, needs, and desires. The question becomes, "Which will most help this young lady become the better person she knows she can be?" The truth is, only she can make that decision.

Our professional occupation is only a tool to help us along the path, and only has value to the extent that it does this.

———⚬⚬⚬———

This is a difficult journey. Along the way there are many barriers and obstacles to be overcome. In the diagram, the symbol @ represents the obstacles that confront us along the way—fear, addiction, discouragement, fatigue, anger, hatred, laziness, and the struggle between good and evil.

Everything in our lives should be seen in relation to this path, and embraced or rejected accordingly. It may seem simple. It may seem over simplified. Genius is the ability to capture complexity with a simple vision. Simplicity is the key to perfection.

The shape, form, and content of our lives is determined by our decisions. Some of them little, some of them large. Each decision impacts not only what we do, but who we become. Life comes down to choices and decisions. We find ourselves constantly at the crossroad.

> *Two roads diverge in a yellow wood,*
> *And sorry I could not travel both*
> *And be one traveler, long I stood*
> *And looked down one as far as I could*
> *To where it bent in the undergrowth;*
>
> *Then took the other, as just as fair,*
> *And having perhaps the better claim,*
> *Because it was grassy and wanted wear;*
> *Though as for that the passing there*
> *Had worn them about the same,*

And both that morning equally lay
In leaves no step had trodden black.
Oh, I kept the first for another day!
Yet knowing how way leads on to way,
I doubted if I should ever come back.

I shall be telling this with a sigh
Somewhere ages and ages hence:
Two roads diverged in a wood, and I—
I took the one less traveled by,
And that has made all the difference.

THE ROAD NOT TAKEN
By Robert Frost

The will of God. It is a concept which exists in almost every religious tradition in history. It is an idea that has been used to manipulate people for centuries. On both sides of every war the troops are told that it is the will of God that they fight, defeat their enemy, and reign victorious.

The will of God is not a plan, schedule, or itinerary. The will of God is an attitude and a disposition.

There is one God, one Divine presence at work in you, in me, and in the whole universe. The will of God is the perfection of creation. God's will for you is that you make the journey from *Point A* to *Point B*. From your journey God gains nothing and I gain nothing. There are a thousand possible paths to walk to achieve this perfection. You must decide which path is best for you. This decision should be based upon your assessment of your legitimate needs, your talents, and your deepest desires.

When we act in ways that are good, true, and noble, they are such—not because "the Bible says so," or because, "it's the law of God." These may very well be the case, but the origins of goodness and truth are much more transcendental and far reaching. God didn't sit down at the beginning of time and write a set of rules for human beings to abide by. God created. By creating in an orderly fashion, certain laws came into being. There is a natural law that does not require a cosmic dictator. The laws are not for God's sake, they are for our sake. They are designed to lead each of us along the path of salvation towards our perfection, so that we can experience the fulfillment that we were created for, and the happiness and peace we desire.

Right and wrong are therefore separated by discerning which action will move you along the path towards being the better person you know you can be. Any action that will lead you along the path will likewise lead others along the path. No action that brings harm to another person will lead you along the path. The most basic spiritual principle is—what you do to another you do to yourself.

It is important, however, to understand that our happiness does not come from reaching *Point B*.

Happiness, a peaceful heart, a tranquil mind, the joy and enthusiasm for life that lead to fulfillment and contentment, are not prizes waiting for us upon arrival at *Point B*. All of these come from the struggle to move toward *Point B*. They are the byproducts of the effort we make to become the better person we know we can be, and they are distributed equally and abundantly at each point along the path.

As we move along the path these fruits—peace, joy, and happiness—slowly sink their roots into the depths of our being. Each day, as we develop the habits that go hand in hand with moving along the path, these roots will move deeper and deeper. As they do, you will become less and less distracted by life's daily troubles, and more and more focused on the path and your development. You will begin to measure your success by what is taking place within you, rather than by what is taking place around you. You will discover a truer assessment of your self-worth. Your self-esteem will grow and you will develop a deep and abiding peace.

This journey is life.

Let me explain it in another way. When you eat well and exercise regularly, how do you feel? Fantastic, yes? What is happening to make you feel that way? You are moving from *Point A* toward *Point B*. Physically, you are growing, changing, developing—becoming the better person you know you can be.

When you fall in love how do you feel? Amazing, energized, inspired, moved, capable of anything. What is happening to make you feel that way? You are moving from *Point A* towards *Point B*. Your ability to love is increasing, your ability to be loved is increasing. Your heart is expanding its capacities. You begin to think of another person before yourself. Emotionally, you are growing, changing, developing—becoming the better person you know you can be.

When you study and learn new truths and ideas, how do you feel? More vital, more vibrant, more alert. Why? You are moving from *Point A* towards *Point B*. Your mind is expanding. Intellectually, you are growing, changing, developing—becoming the better person you know you can be.

When you have a spiritual encounter or experience, how do you feel? Like the whole world could fall apart and it wouldn't matter. Why? Your spirit is expanding and you are beginning to see things with proper perspective and priority. Spiritually, you are growing, changing, developing—becoming the better person you know you can be.

This journey is life. As human beings we respond very well to anything that assists us in making this journey. The human spirit thrives in the midst of this journey and shrivels when this journey is ignored in a person's life.

The best thing you can do for yourself, your family, your friends, your community, your church, your nation, and the world, is to dedicate yourself to this journey.

—⁓—

Develop a strong, uncompromising commitment to becoming the better person you know you can be. Do everything you can to become that person. Enjoy life. Take time each day to visualize that person. If you cannot visualize the better person you wish to become, you cannot become that better person. The more specific your visualization, the faster and more effectively you will be transformed into that better person. Visualize particular ways of acting in certain situations. Visualize them over and over again in your prayer and in the empty moments of the day, and over time they will become a part of your character. All great change and achievement is perceived first in the heart and mind. The first expression of every great achievement has been in the wonder of the imagination. Visualize the changes you wish to achieve. If you do not, you will not.

"Being" is one of the most basic concepts in philosophy. Philosophers hold that the being of something changeable consists not only of what it is, but also of what it still can be—that is, its potential. So, in the philosophical sense of being, as a person you consist not only of who you are now, but also who you are capable of becoming.

It is the vision of the potential within us that leads us to become the better person we know we can be. Recognize your potential. You do not need anything except what is already within you to make this journey.

MINIMALISM

There are certain qualities and attitudes that prevent us from achieving our dreams and becoming the better person we know we can be. Minimalism is one of them. Consciously or subconsciously the minimalist is always asking the question, "What is the least I can do...?"

Minimalism is a mind-set, a habit of the mind, that can affect any area of our lives. What is the least I can do and keep my job? What is the least I can do and still get reasonable grades in school? What is the least I can do and still get to heaven? What is the least I can do and keep my spouse from nagging me? What is the least I can do and stay physically fit? The minimalist wants the fruit of a certain toil, but does not want to toil.

Minimalism breeds mediocrity, and mediocrity is the enemy of excellence, the destroyer of passion.

Minimalism is one of the greatest character diseases of our time. It is an enemy of excellence. It is a cancer on society. The problem is, culturally we encourage minimalism.

—ᴠᴠᴠ—

Our education systems foster, encourage, and reward this attitude. The final exam is the main test of what a student has or has not learned. This allows, if not encourages, students to cram knowledge into their minds for an exam which they will almost immediately forget once the exam has ended. If you pass you move on, if you fail you must repeat the process. At the end of the course you receive a piece of paper ; the reward.

The word education comes from the Latin word *educare* which means, to draw out. We do not teach our children the love of learning. We do not hold knowledge before them as a powerful tool for personal development. We don't produce broadly educated, well-rounded leaders for tomorrow. We teach more and more about less and less. We don't draw out the individual. We impose upon the individual—systems and structures. We don't reverence and treasure individuality, we stifle it and try to stamp it out. We don't educate, we formulate. We abandon the individual in his or her own need and uniqueness, and "impose" the same upon all. We provide an education in specialization. We produce clones for the modern world. We throw people into a mold, which we call an education system, to form cogs for the global economic wheel, all the time dangling the golden carrot before them as incentive and reason.

The truth is, our modern education systems crush the very spirit they claim to instill.

We need to return to the ancient Greek ideal of educating the whole person, and crown that ideal with our modern understanding of spirituality, as we strive to nurture every aspect of the human person—physical, emotional, intellectual, and spiritual.

Minimalism is born from a lack of passion for the things we do. Wherever you find people doing things that they are not passionate about, you will find minimalism.

—ɷɷ—

Our legal systems and our modern interpretation of law are another prime example. Today, people tend to interpret the law in such a way, that they consider whatever they can get away with as right, and whatever they cannot get away with as wrong. In many cases, perhaps not even wrong—just "against the law," or unfortunate.

Speeding is a prime example. The speed limit is fifty-five miles per hour, but you know that the police will not stop you unless you are doing more than sixty-four miles per hour.

The law only obliges us to the minimum.

Once in our system, this diseased mind-set creeps into other areas of our lives, takes a grip of our character, and significantly affects our work and our relationships.

—ɷɷ—

The effects of minimalism are many. Minimalism eats away at the character of a person, and therefore society, just like a disease eats away at the body one cell at a time. The minimalist suffers from dreadfully low self-esteem. His low self-esteem is not the result of failure, but the consequence of not even trying. The minimalist doesn't strive to excel, he strives to survive. The minimalist forgets that it takes just as much energy to avoid excellence as it does to achieve excellence. A person gripped by the mind-set of minimalism becomes very self-seeking and contributes little to the common good of society. The minimalist quickly becomes unfulfilled and miserable, but with no plan to change he goes on, minimally, doing what he has always done and spreading the dissatisfaction and misery that he has created for himself with everyone he meets. The minimalist just goes through the motions. He is a prisoner and victim of the day-to-day drudgery that stifles the greatness of the human spirit.

—◊◊◊—

The truth is that we probably all suffer from minimalism in one form or another. To larger and lesser extents we are all minimalists in different areas of our lives. It is good that we are able to recognize this, because minimalism is like a cancer. It spreads. The good news is, there is a cure for this disease.

In every age there has been a group of people who have escaped and risen above minimalism. These people are successful in many different walks of life. They are achievers, they get the job done. They are legends, heroes, champions, leaders, and saints. They didn't ask themselves, "What is the least I can do...?" and then proceed to lead dispassionate, boring lives of misery and dissatisfaction. Rather, they asked themselves, "What is the most I can do...?" Then, with the vision inspired by this question they set out to do the most they could—the best they could in a single lifetime.

When we look at their lives, we find people who were passionate about what they did, who had a commitment to excellence. They knew how to dream, they were men and women of courage, bold and brilliant people, people who lived exciting lives that leave us simply amazed as we look on as spectators. Their achievements can only be summarized, because they are so many. And the greatness of these achievements will never be fully known to us—or them—for the effects of their achievements continue to impact the lives of people everyday.

Do not ask, "What is the least I can do...?" but rather, in every situation, ask yourself, "What is the most I can do...?" If you are willing, this one question will introduce you to your better self and change your life forever.

Can you imagine an Olympic gold medallist asking herself, "What is the least I can do and still win the gold medal?" Champions don't take short cuts. Champions give everything they have to training, preparation, and competition. That is what makes them champions.

On the day of competition, the day that really counts, every short cut taken in training comes to haunt the athlete.

Building character is a task only for the brave and dedicated. There are no short cuts when it comes to building character. If you wish to cure minimalism in your own life, develop a complete commitment to excellence and an absolute rejection of mediocrity. "What is the most I can do...?" Give this question a permanent place in your inner dialogue, and you will be well on the way to achieving all your dreams and to becoming the better person you know you can be.

ARE YOU FREE?

History has taught us that the one thing men and women have always been prepared to fight for, and indeed die for, is freedom. Freedom is the cornerstone of all great nations. Freedom is the pinnacle of spirituality. And freedom is the most basic and essential human right. While at this time in history there appears to be no threat to our freedom, I believe it is crucially important for us to reassess what makes us free.

What is freedom? This is one of my favorite topics when I speak in high schools. I begin by posing the question to the students and one inevitably replies, "Freedom is when you can do whatever you want, wherever you want, whenever you want, without your parents or teachers telling you to do otherwise."

Consciously or subconsciously, this is how most people view the concept of freedom in the world today. Freedom is viewed as the power, the strength, or merely as the opportunity to choose. This notion is false. Freedom is not the ability to do whatever you want. Freedom is not only the opportunity to choose. Freedom is the strength of character to choose and to do what is right. With that in mind, ours is not an age of freedom, but an age of slavery. It is subtle, but it is real.

The foundation of freedom is not power or choice. Freedom is not upheld by men in government, but by people who govern themselves. Self-discipline is the foundation of freedom. This self-discipline, this mastery of self, is acquired only by the practice of self-denial, and is acquired always from within. Discipline can never be imposed upon a person. It must emerge from within a person.

Self-discipline is the foundation of greatness, achievement, success, heroism, leadership, sanctity, and of vibrant and flourishing communities and nations. There is no liberty where there is no self-discipline.

Speaking in an interview about discipline, Julie Andrews commented, *"Some people regard discipline as a chore. For me, it is a kind of order that sets me free to fly."*

If you examine the lives of men and women who have achieved little or nothing with their lives, people who are miserable, mean, and dispassionate, you will discover that their lives were not destroyed by other people. Destruction always comes from within. It is true for a nation and it is true for individuals.

In 1838, with a prophetic voice, Abraham Lincoln said, *"At what point is the approach of danger to be expected? I answer, if it ever reach us, it must spring up amongst us. It cannot come from abroad. If destruction be our lot, we ourselves must be its author and finisher. As a nation of free men, we must live through all times, or die by suicide."*

On another occasion Lincoln said, *"Our defense is in the preservation of the spirit which prizes liberty as the heritage of all men, in all lands, everywhere. Destroy this spirit, and you have planted the seeds of despotism around your own doors."*

In the later part of the twentieth century we have "planted the seeds of despotism" around our own doors with the creed, message, and motto—"do whatever feels good." In a day and age where there is little real threat of our freedom being attacked by foreign forces, we have become slaves. The threat is not foreign, but local. Very local. Internal. We have become our own worst enemies. The people of these modern times have become slaves to alcohol, drugs, pornography, gambling, sex, violence... Our slavery is the result of a complex of addictions that we often refuse to acknowledge or challenge. These addictions attack and take over not only our bodies, but also our minds, hearts, spirits, and check books.

———

Addiction is the enemy of self-discipline. Addiction is the enemy of freedom. Addiction robs us of self-discipline, freedom, and indeed our very dignity.

During the last five years, I have had the opportunity to travel all over the world and to experience dozens of different cultures. But my fascination lies with the United States. I am continually amazed to witness the impact that America exercises culturally, economically, politically, and socially in literally every country.

The foundation of this nation is the simple, yet practically complex notion of "liberty for all." Freedom! Never was a nation founded on ideals and principles as pure as those the founding fathers laid for this nation. They envisioned a land where men and women could live together in harmony and peace. A prosperous land. A land where the people would help and encourage each other to lead good lives in service of the common good. A land where people would rather help you up than pull you down. A land where dreams could be pursued. A land governed by men and women from all walks of life, with different views, but dedicated to their common purpose of affirming the highest values of the human spirit. Has their vision been realized? Has their dream been forgotten?

The motto "do whatever feels good" and the philosophy "to each their own" are destroying the Founding Fathers' vision and robbing us of our freedom. Such philosophies lead us to have one more beer, or one more shot—because it feels good. These attitudes lead us to cheat on our wives, even if it is her best friend—because it feels good. Then, before you know it, children start walking into classrooms and shooting their teachers and classmates—because it feels good. After a while our children are hungry and have holes in their shoes—because the thrill of gambling feels good. And it goes on, and on, and on.

Where did it all start? Where did we get lost? What went wrong? How do we make it right?

The foundation of great nations is freedom. The foundation of freedom is not strength, but character. The foundation of character is self-discipline.

The moral decay of modern western culture began when we put aside self-discipline, when we stopped expecting it of ourselves, when we failed the tests of friendship, parenthood, and leadership, and stopped expecting it of the people around us.

Our lives and times are plagued with, and characterized by, all types of addictions. We are addicted, and in as much as we are addicted, we are slaves.

We all have addictions. We tend to think of addicts as people who are always high as a kite, or drunken slobs who pass out on the couch every afternoon. Most of us are much better at hiding our addictions. We forget that the true curse of an addiction is not how it affects us externally, but how it affects us internally.

The human spirit is capable of anything and was created to soar. There is nothing more devastating than the stifling of the human spirit.

Addictions take a grip of us from within. They suck the strength from our will and render us useless in any worthwhile cause. The person who is enslaved by addiction has a weak will. Their mind is plagued by doubts, fears, and all manner of negative thoughts. They have no self-control and are not capable of taking the initiative. They follow sheepishly wherever the flock leads. And, they will do anything to avoid taking a good, long, hard look at themselves.

Quite the opposite is a person who is free. The free man or woman is quietly confident and peaceful. Aware of both his strengths and weaknesses, he seeks self-analysis to improve himself. She is a woman of integrity and her word is better than a signed contract. His mind is constantly filled with gratitude, appreciation, and all manner of positive thoughts. She is a leader who is prepared to take the initiative. He is a man of character, self-control, and firm will. She lives by bringing happiness to other people's lives. He has been an addict of one thing or another—perhaps many addictions have plagued his life—but he has overcome them and now guards carefully against new addictions.

Are you free?

—⁓—

I love chocolate. During my time in Austria I was sharing a room with a fine young man from Slovakia named Juraj. One afternoon I was having a rest after a hectic day of classes. When he came into the room I was lying on my bed, reading and eating a large bar of chocolate. He said to me, "I think you eat too much chocolate." I humored him and admitted that he was probably right. Then he said, "Are you free from it?" I looked at him as if to say, "What are you talking about?" He saw that thought on my face and asked again, "Really, are you free from it?" He then picked up a book from his desk and left the room.

I immediately began to think about it more. I could not answer that question. I didn't know if I was free from chocolate. It was such a regular part of my life. So, I decided to answer that question in the only way I knew how. I decided from that day on, I would not have any chocolate for one month.

Then it began. The excuses and the crying out of the body, those tormenting urges that demand to be satisfied. I lasted about sixty hours before I found myself devouring a large bar of chocolate. The next day I resolved to try again. Three times I failed. The fourth time I was able to give up chocolate for over three months. Then, and only then, I knew I was free from chocolate. I knew it was my servant, not my master.

I discovered that chocolate had become a part of my everyday. Now it is an occasional joy in my life, and I enjoy it more than I did when I was eating a pound at a time as part of my everyday routine. I taste it now. It sounds silly, but I don't even remember really tasting it back then.

If you think you are addicted to something, there is only one way to find out. They say twenty-one days is the critical time period for breaking addictions. Say no to it. If you can, you are not addicted. If you cannot, then there is a good chance you are.

—◁◈▷—

Aldous Huxley observed, *"Addiction is an increasing desire for an act which gives less and less satisfaction."*

We all have addictions. Some are much more serious than an addiction to chocolate, but the effect is the same. Addictions weaken the will, which weakens our character, which weakens our ability to achieve and succeed in every other area of our lives. Every area of life is weakened by addiction. Mahatma Ghandi once wrote, *"Man cannot do right in one department of life whilst he is occupied in doing wrong in another department. Life is one indivisible whole."*

How do we acquire these addictions? We become addicted simply by taking the path of least resistance. We live by the mottoes, "Do whatever feels good" and "What is the least I can do?" In doing so, we begin to form certain habits. In forming these habits we become addicted to certain patterns of behavior that are ultimately self-destructive.

We are creatures of habit. I do not know why. Nonetheless, knowing this we should use this self-knowledge to our advantage. We can achieve this by forming habits that lead us to become the better person we know we can be.

If a child learns to quit every time he is unsuccessful, his character will never bear the jewel of perseverance. He will form the self-destructive habit of quitting. If a person's character is scarred by this trait, what will he achieve in life? Nothing. Likewise, if a young girl learns to be patient with her little brother, even though he is slower and clumsier, she will quickly develop the empowering habit of patience. When this young lady comes up against obstacles in life, her habitual response will be patient perseverance. If a person's character is marked with this trait, what will she achieve in life? Great things. We are indeed creatures of habit.

—⁓—

Addictions are acquired by practicing a certain type of behavior often and excessively. Character is acquired by practicing certain types of behavior often and excessively.

We break addictions in the same way we form them. An addiction is a pattern of behavior. It is not enough merely to give up a certain type of self-destructive behavior. In its place we must form a self-empowering habit. It is of course much more difficult to break an addiction than to form one. To become addicted to something, one must merely follow the path of least resistance—doing whatever feels good. To overcome an addiction, one must choose that which is true, right, noble, and good—against the tormenting urges of the senses which are constantly demanding satisfaction. To overcome addictions we must first realize and admit that we have lost control of that particular area of our life, and admit that the addiction has become a self-destructive habit.

To overcome an addiction you need a certain clarity of ideas. This clarity comes from knowing that the change is desirable. Desire is the greatest motivator. If you can see how overcoming the addiction will give you a richer, fuller life, and constantly remind yourself of this fact, your desire for a richer, fuller life will become greater than your desire for the addictive behavior.

To overcome an addiction you must see it in relation to the path, the journey from *Point A* to *Point B*.

Addictions stifle our personal development. They prevent us from changing, growing, and becoming the better person we know we can be. With this realization we need a strategy. There has been no strategy for overcoming addictions more successful than the twelve step program of *Alcoholics Anonymous*. And, although it is not a guide to overcoming and recovering from all types of addiction, it gives us an idea of the type of strategy needed to overcome an addiction. The program was developed by two alcoholics. The program is the story, witness, and testimony of their struggle to overcome their addiction to alcohol. It is a story that has guided and inspired millions to seek freedom from that same addiction. It is a lengthy program, but is based on these twelve simple steps:

Step One

We admitted we were powerless over alcohol—that our lives had become unmanageable.

Step Two

Came to believe that a Power greater than ourselves could restore us to sanity.

Step Three

Made a decision to turn our will and our lives over to the care of God *as we understood Him*.

Step Four

Made a searching and fearless moral inventory of ourselves.

Step Five

Admitted to God, to ourselves, and to another human being the exact nature of our wrongs.

Step Six

Were entirely ready to have God remove all these defects of character.

Step Seven

Humbly asked Him to remove our shortcomings.

Step Eight

Made a list of all persons we had harmed, and became willing to make amends to them all.

Step Nine

Made direct amends to such people wherever possible, except when to do so would injure them or others.

Step Ten

Continued to take personal inventory and when we were wrong promptly admitted it.

Step Eleven

Sought through prayer and meditation to improve our conscious contact with God *as we understood Him*, praying only for knowledge of His will for us and the power to carry that out.

Step Twelve

Having had a spiritual awakening as a result of these steps, we tried to carry this message to alcoholics, and to practice these principles in all our affairs.

—⁓—

We should remind ourselves that addiction is not confined to areas such as alcohol, drugs, or gambling. The reality is, we all have addictions. Some of them large and serious problems, others small and minor problems. Whatever the addiction, the effect is the same. Addictions drain us of our will power and make cowards of us all. Some people are addicted to having the remote control in their hand when they are watching television. Take it from them, and their reaction will have addiction written all over it. Some people cannot survive, they think, without coffee first thing in the morning. Others are addicted to having everything in their house, office, and car exactly in the right place and perfectly tidy. Others are addicted to cigarettes. The point is, we all have addictions—habits that enslave us. There are areas of our lives that have become OUT OF CONTROL. Areas in our lives where externals determine how we act and what we do—areas of our lives where we are not masters of ourselves.

What areas of your life have become out of control?

In the beginning we form our habits. After a while they begin to form us. If we do not conquer our bad habits, sooner or later, they conquer us.

—⁓—

The Rhythm of Life maximizes our efficiency and well-being by creating a certain balance and harmony between the four major elements of our being—physical, emotional, intellectual, and spiritual. Addictions are a serious drain on our efficiency and effectiveness. Addictions do not affect only one area of our lives, they affect our whole lives, because life is one. They deprive us of our well-being and rob us of our personal freedom.

All true spirituality seeks to free us from any type of slavery which prevents us from moving along the path and becoming a more loving and more lovable person. A valuable exercise to make a regular part of our prayer, reflection, and self-analysis, is to seek out and identify areas of addiction and slavery in our lives.

I find myself agreeing with Charles Dickens when he wrote, *"I only ask to be free. The butterflies are free."*

FOLLOW YOUR STAR

It was not the chief priests, or even the high priest of that year, that recognized the signs that accompanied the coming of Jesus. But rather, it was the three Magi who recognized these signs. The star rose in the east and they followed the star.

One Christmas, a couple of years back, I was driving past a church on the east coast of America and outside was one of those message boards. It read, *"Wise men still seek Jesus today."* That simple message had an impact on me and I have often taken time to reflect on it. My reflection leads me to ask these questions: What was the difference between the Magi and everybody else on the planet at the time the Messiah made his entrance into the world? What was the difference between the three wise men and the chief priests?

When someone shares a remarkable piece of knowledge, you will sometimes hear people say, "Oh, isn't she wise." There is an enormous difference between knowledge and wisdom. The chief priests had knowledge. They could have told you every single passage that related to the coming of the Messiah, including the place of his birth. The Magi didn't have anywhere near as much knowledge as the chief priests regarding the coming of the Christ, but what they did know they lived by. That is why we call the Magi the wise men, and the chief priests, the chief priests.

Wisdom is not the amassing of knowledge. Wisdom is truth lived.

—◊◊◊—

The scriptures do not tell us how old the Magi were, nor are we told how long they had been following the star. However, one thing is certain—it takes time to develop the understanding and awareness necessary to recognize your star when it rises. The Magi had probably been waiting and preparing for many years.

The first lesson in finding and following your own personal star is patience. Many people lose their chance at greatness by chasing after the first star that rises.

We should prepare patiently for our star to rise. It will not rise early. It will not rise late. It will rise in the fullness of time—at the most appropriate time. You need not worry that you will not be ready. It will not rise until you are. You should not fear that you will miss it, or not recognize it. It will help you to fulfill the purpose of your existence and your whole life is leading you toward it.

As you wait for your star to rise there is much preparation to be done. Dreams come true when opportunity and preparation meet. Now is your time to prepare. Do not say, "I am too old." Do not say, "I am too young." Now is your time to prepare. You are where you are right now for a reason, reading what you are reading for a reason.

—⁓—

During this time of preparation you must search your heart and grow to know intimately your talents, your needs, and your desires. When your star does rise, you will know it is your star because you will have a burning desire to follow that star—not on a whim, but through careful consideration. In following that star you will put your talents to use for the service of others and for your own fulfillment and satisfaction. This employment of your talents will lead to the fulfillment of all your legitimate needs—physical, emotional, intellectual, and spiritual—and help others to fulfill their legitimate needs.

Since my teenage years I have been fascinated with famous and extraordinary people—great achievers in all walks of life. I love to watch them being interviewed. I love to watch footage of their day-to-day lives. One thing that has always struck me, and I do not consider it in the slightest way to be coincidental, is that great men and women always believed that they were destined to be great.

From this day on begin to foster a belief that you were born for a reason, and although you may not have yet discovered that reason, you are being prepared for it and led toward it.

In general terms, you know that your purpose is to grow, change, develop, and become the better person you know you are capable of being. It is this *process of growth* that makes life interesting, exciting, rewarding, and fulfilling.

Dedication to this process of growth is greatness. Greatness should never be confused with fame, fortune, status, or power. These things are only passing illusions. Greatness is to be true to yourself.

A chance for greatness awaits you—your own personal chance at greatness—and it will involve the unique and providential blend of your talents, needs, and desires. The pursuit of your chance at greatness will reveal you to your family, friends, colleagues, spouse, children, and everyone who crosses your path. It is the attuning of your personality. Life is a revelation of self. Life is a story, your life is your story. Life is for you—and yet, in a paradoxical but complimentary way, it is also your chance to serve your neighbor, to touch and enrich others, and to make a difference in this sometimes weary world. This is the way of God—to lead you toward your perfection and fulfillment, while at the same time using your journey to lead others toward their perfection and fulfillment.

—◦◦◦—

The right circumstances will emerge. I prefer to think of them as opportunities. The right opportunities will emerge. Circumstances hatch opportunities which enable us to follow our star. The circumstances of our lives often perfectly and providentially prepare us to follow our star. Charlie is a great example.

Charlie Chaplin was born into a very poor family in London. While Charlie was still very young his father left his mother and their poverty was exaggerated. Mrs. Chaplin couldn't find work, couldn't pay the rent, couldn't afford fuel to heat their small apartment, and most nights Charlie and his brother ate fish head soup. Nothing but the heads of fish in warm water with a little bread. Miserable circumstances, I'm sure you'd agree.

From that misery was born one of the greatest talents humanity has ever known. Charlie Chaplin developed his humor and comedy to rise above those depressing circumstances. He put together all types of acts to make his mother and brother laugh. He later recalled wanting to make them laugh so much that they would forget how desperately hungry they were.

By 1918 Charlie Chaplin was 29 years old and indisputably the most famous man in the world. He continued to write and direct until his death in Vevey, Switzerland, on Christmas day in 1977. Over a lifetime he wrote and directed 81 films, founded his own studios in California, and made more people laugh than anyone else in history. Charlie Chaplin is a legend. He followed his star. The circumstances of his childhood prepared him to recognize the star when it rose, and rise it did.

—⟿—

Following your star is about discovering who you are and what you are capable of. Following your star is about learning to be yourself. You must be prepared to dare to be different in a world where uniformity is safe and rewarded.

Search yourself. Discover something deep within that is yours and no one else's.

Uncover your uniqueness.

Your chance at greatness is intrinsically linked to being yourself. Become a champion of selfhood and you will certainly excel in all you do.

Everyone is good at something. We all have talents and abilities that are unique and different. These gifts are the key to great happiness in our lives, and on occasion are leading indicators in the search to discover our vocation or mission in life. But first we must seek out these gifts and talents. So often people say to me, "But I am not good at anything." This I cannot believe. I can believe, however, that a person has not yet found that one area in which he or she has a special gift.

Frustration and the sense of failure tend to follow us wherever we go until we find our own area in which to work, our own gift to develop, our own niche. Don't despair. Have a little faith. It can take some time, but the active search brings a sense of fulfillment in the interim. It is only when we give up the search, believing that we will never find that special talent, or that we simply do not possess one, that frustration and depression take their hold on us.

Hold firm. The search is noble. Avoiding the search is cowardice.

Sometimes we think we have found that special talent and what we have found is only a stepping stone. Six years ago I was studying at University in Australia toward a degree in business with a major in marketing. I thought I had found my gift. I was wrong. It was just a stepping stone. My true gift I now believe is my speaking and my writing. Was the time I spent studying business a waste of time? Absolutely not. I can clearly see the hand of God in that part of my life. In many indirect ways God was preparing me then for what I am doing now. In the future it may be revealed to me that this is just another stepping stone to something else, somewhere else.

George Washington was first a surveyor. For many years Norman Vincent Peale was a newspaper man. Garth Brooks wasn't always a musician. Peter was first a fisherman, Matthew a tax collector. Sting was first a school teacher. Harrison Ford was a carpenter. Before Somerset Maughan began writing, he graduated from medical school. John Denver worked for an insurance company before embarking on his journey to become an international acclaimed entertainer and songwriter.

—⁓—

As you seek out your dominant talent, it is important to remember that everyone wasn't born to be in the spotlight. Here are two of this century's greatest examples.

Do you know who Brian Epstein is? Do you know who the Beatles are? At lunchtime on November 9, 1961 Brian Epstein walked into a dark, crowded, smoky club in his hometown of Liverpool, England. The club was called *The Cavern* and Epstein had gone there to hear a local group, four young men who called themselves *The Beatles*.

At that time Brian Epstein managed and operated a small record store which his father owned. His curiosity was piqued when in one day, six people came in asking for *The Beatles* record. When he tried to order the record, he discovered no such record existed. This is what drew him to *The Cavern*.

Two weeks later, Epstein offered to manage the Beatles. He confessed to them that he had no experience, but that he truly believed they had what it took to be "the next big thing." The Beatles agreed, despite his lack of experience, to let him manage them—John Lennon later recalled, "We had nothing to lose. We had already been turned down by every major recording label in the country. He was enthusiastic about us and our music. We had everything to gain, and nothing to lose."

So for the next seven months Brian Epstein went knocking on doors in London, playing the demo tape for every recording company he could get to listen. They all said the same things, "These boys will never make it," or, "It just won't work," and, "Their sound is just too different." Epstein's reply to each of them was, "These boys are going to be bigger than Elvis." They just laughed at him. At the time, this was an altogether absurd claim. Elvis was at the peak of his popularity and a British group hadn't made it big in America for years.

Finally, in June of 1962 he broke through. The Beatles recorded their first session at the EMI studios in London—two songs, *Love Me Do* and *P.S. I Love You.*

The Beatles' first British record was released on September 11, 1962 and entered the charts forty eight hours later at number forty-nine. It peaked a couple of weeks later at number seventeen and the Beatles had their first top twenty hit with *Please. Please, Me.*

The door was open and before too long they had a record succession of British number one hits. From there they took Europe by storm, and in no time word spread to Asia, America, and Australia as the anticipation of their world tour began to build.

The Beatles came to the United States for the first time on February 7th in 1964, and although by that time they had reached a certain level of fame in Europe, nothing could have prepared them for what was about to happen. When the Beatles stepped off the plane on that early February morning there were 10,000 screaming fans at New York's John F. Kennedy Airport to meet them. Whether they were aware of it or not, their lives changed forever that day.

By May of that same year, *The Beatles* had become a worldwide phenomenon, like nothing in any of our lifetimes, like nothing we will ever see again. And yes, they had become bigger than Elvis.

The absurd had become a reality.

When their fifth record, *Can't Buy Me Love*, was released in America, it went immediately into the number one position on the charts, topping five other Beatles records that were occupying the first five places on the charts. Are we ever again likely to see a group occupy the first six places on a Billboard chart?

Who was Brian Epstein? He was the man of insight, passion, courage, vision, integrity, fortitude, and marketing genius—the friend, manager, uniting force, and tireless worker who made *The Beatles* the worldwide phenomenon that they were, and the historical legends that they will always remain.

He believed that they were something special and because of his belief the world came to know *The Beatles*.

Perhaps your talent is to help others find and share their talents.

—⁓—

Today, sports agents, endorsements, and sports management are all a big thing, but it wasn't always so. In fact, forty years ago they didn't exist. What changed to bring about this whole culture of sporting celebrities, sports agents, and incredible endorsements? Let me tell you, all of this is the result of one man following his own personal star.

In 1960 Mark McCormack was a reasonably successful marketing executive in Cleveland. In November of that same year he saw a young man play golf in a way he had never seen anyone play. It wasn't just his swing, it wasn't just the way he struck the ball, it was everything. And not the least of which was this young man's personality.

McCormack looked into this young golfer's eyes and he saw the potential for greatness. On that day Mark McCormack saw his star rising. He had a vision. He saw something that was not yet, but that could be. Some people said McCormack's vision was impossible. Mc-Cormack said it was inevitable. He approached the young golfer and inquired as to whether or not he had a manager. The golfer told him that no such person existed in his life, and McCormack offered to fill the gap.

Filling gaps has made more people successful and rich than anything else. You could call it freak chance—I prefer to think of it as preparation meeting opportunity.

The young golfer's name was Arnold Palmer. He became Mark McCormack's first client. That day the concept and organization now known as International Management Group, or IMG, was founded. IMG's first three clients were Arnold Palmer, Gary Player, and Jack Nicholas. These three golfers began to win everything and in time became the famed "Big Three."

Today IMG has offices in sixty countries, more than two-thousand employees, and represent Pete Sampras, Joe Montana, Wayne Gretzky, supermodels Niki Taylor and Tyra Banks, Formula One driver Michael Schumacher, Itzhak Pearlman, Michael Johnson, Andre Agassi, Nick Faldo and more than one-third of the top thirty golfers in the world.

For thirty consecutive years IMG's first client, Arnold Palmer, was the highest-grossing athlete in the world in terms of income from endorsements. Only in 1991, at age sixty-four, was he surpassed by Michael Jordan. Arnold Palmer still ranks second.

It all began with one man following his star.

It takes a little time sometimes to really find that one ability and talent that makes you unique and special. Don't give up the search.

—⁓—

If you have heard me speak, you know of my great love for stories. There is something very powerful about stories. Each listener hears something different according to their own place on the journey. Stories help us discover who we are and who we can be. Stories are important. To poison a person, poison the stories you tell him. To demoralize a person, tell her demoralizing stories. You will always be as confident and healthy as the stories you read, listen to, and tell yourself. We become the stories we listen to, read, and tell. That is the power of a story. Conrad Hilton, the founder of Hilton Hotels, used to tell this story.

A very poor Greek once applied for a job as a janitor in a bank in Athens. "Can you write?" demanded the discriminating head of employment. "Only my name," said the fellow. He didn't get the job—so he borrowed the required money to travel steerage to the United States, the "land of opportunity."

Many years later an important Greek businessman held a press conference in his beautiful Wall Street offices. At the conclusion, an enterprising reporter said, "You should write your memoirs." The gentleman smiled. "Impossible," he said, "I cannot write." The reporter was astounded. "Just think," he remarked, "how

much further you would have gone if you could write."
The Greek shook his head and said, "If I could write, I'd
be a janitor."

—∿∿—

Follow your star. Wait for it to rise. While you are waiting, prepare yourself. Become intimately familiar with
your talents, needs, and desires. Remember, circumstances are opportunities. Then, when you see a star
rise on the horizon of your life, and you are filled with
a burning desire to follow it, and you perceive that by
following it you will use your talents and fulfill your
legitimate needs—follow it. Once you begin to follow
it, let nothing distract you from it.

Every legend, hero, leader, champion, and saint in history has followed his or her own personal star. In doing
so, they have grasped their chance at greatness—and
left the people around them awe-inspired and amazed.

THERE IS ONLY ONE YOU

It may sound absurd, but it is true. Most people spend
their whole lives running away from themselves or
hiding themselves from others. I believe that life should
be a process of self-revelation. As we live, we reveal ourselves to the people we love and to the people that cross
our path along the way. We can put up barriers and put
on masks, or we can let people see us as we really are.

What concerns us about the latter is that others might
see our faults. In our concern we forget that we all have
faults. The people who are able to love and admire us
have faults and flaws. The people who criticize and
express anger and hatred towards us have flaws and fail-

ings. As human beings our common bond is our broken-ness. It is a great wisdom to be able to see yourself in other people. It is this insight that empowers us to love every-one, everywhere, at all times, and in all circumstances.

We all want to be liked and accepted. The danger which emerges from this desire, is that we may fall into the trap of doing things or saying things just to please others. Each time we walk this path we abandon a por-tion of our *self*. There is a part of each of us which is weak and can be bought. There is also a part of each of us which is strong and cannot be bought at any price. Decrease the former. Increase and nurture the latter. Befriend the latter, it will tell you who you are.

The truth is, nobody is loved by everybody. Even the greatest men and women in history have detractors and critics. Even people who have dedicated themselves and their lives selflessly to assist others have critics and detractors. You are no different. Some people are going to like you, some people are going to love you, some people are not going to like you at all, and some people may even despise you. You might as well be yourself. That way, at least you will know that the people who like you, like you for who you are.

—⁓—

The great men and women of every age that we have and will speak of throughout this book—the legends and saints that fill our history books, the heroes and champions that fill our hearts and minds with inspira-tion—all listened to their own inner voices of need, desire, and talent.

Their greatness was not the result of luck, or freak chance. They were not singled out at the beginning of time to be special or favored. They laid the foundation of character and listened to these inner voices. Then with passion, belief, commitment, courage, and perseverance, they followed their star.

Their lives reveal the secrets of love, success, achievement, heroism, leadership, and holiness. It would be a mistake to imitate what one of these men and women did with his or her life. It would be a mistake *not* to imitate "the way" they lived their lives. The difference may seem subtle, but it is great. The spirit by which they lived should be imitated, but you have your own path to walk and your own star to follow. Imagine if Beethoven had tried to be another Mozart, or if Picasso had tried to be another Michelangelo. What beauty and wonder will you deny the world if you abandon your *self*?

This chapter has been an exercise in discovering who we are as individuals. Every happiness in life comes from discovering who you are as a unique individual and being true to your *self*.

The following is a brief passage from the diary of Dag Hammarskjold.

"At every moment you choose yourself. But do you choose your self? Body and soul contain a thousand possibilities out of which you can build many I's. But in only one of them is there a congruence of the elector and the elected. Only one—which you will never find until you have excluded all those superficial and fleeting possibilities of being and doing with which you toy, out of curiosity or wonder or greed, and which hinder you from casting anchor in the experience of the mystery of life, and the consciousness of the talent entrusted to you which is your I."

—∿∿—

Who are you? In many different ways people try to discover who they truly are as individuals. Some go off into the mountains, some travel to distant lands, others go to monasteries and convents, some walk up and down the beach early each morning, and others yet, seek to discover themselves through writing or music. I have even heard people use "finding themselves" as an excuse for leaving their husband or wife. You may try any path you wish. You may try to find yourself in a thousand different ways, but in a wonderfully profound and mysterious way, it is only through self-donation—giving ourselves to others—that we discover our true *self*.

There is no greater gift than the sincere gift of self. It is the essence of relationship and life.

It is not something that I completely understand, nor is it something I can clearly and definitively explain. But at the times in my life when I have been able to summon the strength of character it takes to give of my time, energy, and resources to make a difference in other people's lives—I have experienced an unquenchable happiness and satisfaction.

Perhaps this story, which I am told Bruce Barton used to tell, will help illustrate my point.

There are two seas in Palestine. One is fresh and fish are in it. Splashes of green adorn its banks. Trees spread their branches over it and stretch out their thirsty roots to sip its healing waters.

Along its shores the children play, as children played when He was there. He loved it. He could look across its silver surface when He spoke His parables. And on rolling plain not far away He fed five thousand people. The river Jordan makes this sea with sparkling water from the hills. So it laughs in the sunshine. And men build their houses near to it, and birds their nests, and every kind of life is happier because it is there.

The river Jordan flows on south into another sea.

Here, there is no splash of fish, no fluttering leaf, no song of birds, no children's laughter. Travelers choose another route, unless on urgent business. The air hangs heavy above its water, and neither man nor beast nor fowl will drink.

What makes this mighty difference in these two seas? Not the river Jordan. It empties the same good water into both. Not the soil in which they lie; and not the country that surrounds them.

This is the difference. The Sea of Galilee receives, but does not keep the Jordan. For every drop that flows into it another drop flows out. The giving and receiving go on in equal measure.

The other sea is shrewder, hoarding its income jealously. It will not be tempted into any generous impulse. Every drop it gets, it keeps.

The Sea of Galilee gives and lives. The other sea gives nothing. It is named The Dead.

There are two kinds of people in the world; there are two seas in Palestine.

—~~~—

There is more to life than getting, grabbing, having and receiving. Life is as much about giving as it is about receiving. Give of yourself. The meaning of life is mysteriously revealed in this act.

This chapter has been dedicated to the adventure of self-discovery. I hope it is the beginning of a journey that lasts your whole lifetime.

You are different. Not better, just different. Unique and special. A wonder and a marvel. Be all you can be. Be yourself.

CHAPTER 4

THE IMPORTANCE OF RHYTHM

RHYTHM, HARMONY, AND PEACE

There is a natural rhythm to life. Every element of creation has its own unique rhythm. The seasons have their cycles—the darkness, death, and cold of winter give way to the warmth, joy, and new life of springtime. The universe finds rhythm through time. The darkness gives birth to the light of a new day as the sun rises in the east, and then, at the end of each day, the sunset surrenders us to rest. The waves crash on the beaches and the tides rise and fall attuned to a rhythm. The whole process of growth, development, and fruition of plants—photosynthesis—is centered around a rhythm. Our hearts beat to a rhythm, pumping our very life blood around our bodies. And particularly, rhythm is the key to the powerful role a woman's body plays in reproduction. The rhythm brings forth life. Creation is ordered by rhythm. Rhythm is important.

All the elements of nature were created in harmony. As I ponder the mysterious realities of nature, they remind me of a greater overall plan. I can then appreciate the harmonious workings of the universe as one whole, despite the apparent chaos. I find comfort in the rhythm and harmony of nature. In nature, despite its complexity and vastness, there is rhythm, and the rhythm creates harmony.

If we can discover the rhythm of our own lives, that rhythm will in turn create a harmony and balance that will give birth to a deep and abiding peace. And it is that peace, the fruit of harmony, that allows the highest levels of effective and abundant living.

—∼∼—

Perhaps you have heard of the king of ancient times who, so inflated with pride, thought he could hold the tide back simply by commanding it to do so. After all, the tides were part of "his kingdom" and therefore subject to his rule. Late one night the king gave orders for his throne to be placed at the water's edge during low tide. Early the next morning the king went to the beach and sat on his thrown. Just before sunrise the people of his kingdom began to crowd the beach. As the sun came up so did the tide. The king commanded the tide to recede but his command was ignored. Not willing to have his reputation damaged, the king drowned commanding the tide to recede.

—∿∿—

You cannot hold the tide back. Nature has an unmatched strength and persistence. Wisdom is to harness the strength of our own better nature by working with it; by discovering and adopting *The Rhythm of Life*.

If only we could develop an understanding of our nature as human beings and harness the power of that nature by working with its strength. It is then that unimaginable achievements would be recognized in our lives.

We must learn the lesson nature has to teach us. Nature's message can be seen and heard each and every day, "Great things are achieved little by little. Discover *The Rhythm of Life* and develop your life around this rhythm, and peace and prosperity will be yours."

The truth of this message is displayed innumerable times everyday. The waves roll into the shore, washing against the rocks, and an erosion occurs. You do not see it with the first wave, nor with the second or third, but over the years you realize that slowly and steadily the waves are wearing the rock down. Who would think of water as stronger than rock? Strength through persistence.

The Rhythm of Life is a powerful thing.

FINDING OUR PLACE IN CREATION

The creation narratives from the Judeo-Christian scriptures offer some profound insights as we seek to understand our place in creation.

There is order to all of creation. Despite the constant change, there is order and consistency. Everything was created in harmony. This order and harmony are in some way a reflection of God's own personal qualities. Creation is a message from God. Creation is a natural revelation. In every instance God's work reveals something of God, and in every revelation there is a lesson for humanity.

Two of the valuable insights we gain as we read the account of creation in *Genesis* is the rhythm God intended for our lives and our place in creation.

———

On the first day God created light, He separated the light from the darkness and called the light day and the darkness night. Then He reflected on His work and saw that it was good.

On the second day God made a vault to divide the waters of heaven from the waters of earth.

On the third day He created the dry land and filled it with trees and plants, and all types of vegetation. Then He reflected on His work and saw that it was good.

On the fourth day He placed lights in the heavens "to divide day from night" and to "indicate festivals, days, and years." Then He reflected on His work and saw that it was good.

On the fifth day He filled the sea and the air with all types of creatures. Then He reflected on His work and saw that it was good.

On the sixth day God created the animals of the earth, the man, and the woman. Then He reflected on His work and saw that it was good.

"Thus the heavens and the earth were finished, and all their multitude. And on the seventh day God finished the work that He had done, and He rested on the seventh day from all the work that He had done. So God blessed the seventh day and hallowed it, because on it God rested from all the work that He had done."

———

One by one, each day of creation reveals another level of humanity's dependence on the other elements of nature. We are dependent on the sun for light and energy. We are dependent on water. We are dependent on trees for fresh air, and plants and vegetation for food and nourishment.

Humanity is dependent on the other elements of nature. It makes sense that God created us dependent on them, so that we would not abuse and destroy these other elements of creation. Perhaps the idea in the mind of God was, if we were dependent on them we would respect and live in harmony with them. Maybe God did this to lead us to the clues and to show us how closely linked we are, and must remain, to the rest of creation.

From this narrative of creation I wish to draw attention to two themes: our dependency on the other elements of nature, and the institution of rest as a Divine pastime.

———

The actions of God so often are a response to the needs of humanity. On the seventh day God rested. God did not need to rest. He did, however, foresee our need for rest. And in foreseeing our need for rest he established the Sabbath, *The Seventh Day*, as a holy day—to be set aside for rest and renewal.

By creating the Sabbath, by setting this time apart, God provided another tool to restore and maintain rhythm in our lives—the rhythm that restores the balance, harmony, and peace intended for us.

In Chapter Five we will discuss in detail *The Seventh Day* as an instrument for creating and maintaining *The Rhythm of Life*.

—⁓—

The Rhythm of Life leads us to a deeper understanding of ourselves and our place and role in nature, empowering us to harness our own natural energies.

PRIORITIES

Do you ever feel that if you weren't so busy you could be happier, more fulfilled, more effective, and maybe even a better person? Often in my life I have had this sense, and yet, until recently, so rarely have I done anything substantial about it. Our lives have a habit of gathering a momentum of their own.

In a very real way, our lifestyles are a reflection of our priorities.

One of the strange and false ideas that is propagated in the modern world is that an important and successful person is always busy. Another of those strange ideas is that material success is the measure of greatness. Many people judge, and are judged, by how busy they are and how much money they earn. The result is that many rush around in a frenzy, dressed in designer label clothes, trying to give the appearance that they are busy and earning a lot of money—after all, these are the signs of success!

The cost of such a lifestyle is the loss of the necessary consistency and rhythm in our lives. The cost of this type of success is often the loss or failure to find one's very *self*—our truest and deepest desires, talents, dreams, needs, and the necessary pursuit of these. Sadly, with our focus so firmly fixed on these other less important, almost inconsequential things, many of us are completely unaware of what we have lost or are missing.

We need to dedicate ourselves to our development as a person—body, heart, mind, and soul. There is nothing more important in life. I know it, you know it, but we let the things we *do* get in the way. We get carried away with doing. We become human doings. Life is about being and becoming. We must remind ourselves continually that there is nothing more important than our development as human beings.

———

I used to think I was busy, but then I met one or two people who were really busy. The thing I learned from these people who truly did have an enormous amount of work and responsibility is that they have order, they have rhythm. They know their priorities and resist sacrificing their health—physically, emotionally, intellectually, or spiritually—merely for a couple of hours extra work, or a few more dollars.

Rhythm and order create harmony and efficiency.

—⌇ʌʌ⌇—

We do, of course, live in a time which is marked by tremendous technological advancement. Every time saving device is available to us and still no one has time.

Each morning my assistant presents me with a list of things that he thinks should be attended to that day. The list includes phone calls to be made, letters to be written, meetings to attend, as well as my travel schedule. On top of those things I need to set time apart to pray, write, exercise, and to stay in touch with family and friends. Everyday I go through the list and say to something, "I won't have time to do that today." In itself, that is fine. Nobody can do everything. What is critical is what I decide to exclude and why I decide to exclude it.

When was the last time you said, "I don't have time!" either to an idea in your mind, or to a person? What was it that you didn't have time to do? For most people it is something like spending time with the family, or taking the time to look up an old friend and make sure that life is not treating her too harshly. For others it is exercise, or that extra time it takes to eat properly. And at one point or another, for all of us, it is prayer. And yet, if God appeared to you right now in a vision and told you that three weeks from today you would be making the journey from this life to the next, would you rush back to work to make your millions? Would you rush out to the mall to make sure you had the right clothes to die in? No. Most of us would spend time with family and friends, and in some way, try to prepare ourselves for that journey to the next life.

We do not know how long our lives on this earth will last. Some things are more important than others.

Prayer, reflection, meditation, and a life with rhythm, remind us of this truth and help us to remain focused on the things that are really important.

—m—

In my life I have found many things. As a boy I once found a beautiful soccer ball in the park just down the road from our home in Sydney. When I arrived home with the ball my mother inquired as to where it had come from. I told her I had found it. She asked, "Where did you find it?" and I told her, "Down at the park." Then she said to me, "Did it occur to you that someone might come back for it, or that the person who has lost it is very sad right now?" She paused, then continued, "How would you feel if that was your soccer ball and you had lost it?"

I sat in a big green arm chair in the corner of the dining room with the ball grasped to my chest while a few minutes of that deadly silence passed—the silence that even as a child you know means you have done something not altogether right. My mother kept about her business in the kitchen preparing dinner, and then, knowing she had given me just enough time to think about the situation said, "I think you should take the ball back to the park now and leave it where you found it."

After that I found other things. One day I found a watch, and, at a carnival once I found fifty dollars. But I have never found time. It just never happens. Sometimes people ask us, "When are you going to do this?" or, "When are you going to do that?" I have discovered that when my reply to these questions is, "When I find time!" I never do those things. I never find that time.

Even as a child I learned quickly that from the moment we are born into this life and placed on this planet there is more to do than can ever be done, more to see than can ever be seen, and if something is important we must make time.

We must decide what is really important, really necessary, make it a priority, and make time. Otherwise the siren call of the world will always keep us busy and distracted from what really is important. What really counts?

There is a short prayer that I like to use often during the day, particularly during busy times. "God, help me to see that so few things are really important, and to at least take care of these first."

—◦◦◦—

Our priorities should not be based on a material goal. Rather, we should use our time and our talents to develop our whole person—physically, emotionally, intellectually, and spiritually. Our personal development should be our top priority. When we are fully alive, in every way, striving toward perfection, we experience the profound joy of life.

Finding *The Rhythm of Life* is largely about reassessing our priorities and reallocating our resources and energies physically, emotionally, intellectually, and spiritually according to those new priorities. The result is the whole person, a person fully alive, striving to grow, develop, and perfect the various aspects of our character.

TIMING

One of my great childhood loves was golf, and although I do not get many opportunities to play these days, what

I learned on the golf course through my mid-teenage years has had a lasting impact on my life. That knowledge seems to constantly have new applications.

Golf is a lot like life. If you are a golfer, you may know what I mean. If you are not a golfer, you may just want to pass me off as another obsessed sporting fanatic. But, let me explain.

You can never have a perfect round of golf. There is always that shot that you could have hit a little further, or a little straighter. The secret to successful golf is tempo, timing, rhythm.

When a shot doesn't go exactly as you wanted it to, you must control the disappointment and frustration. Otherwise, it will affect your next shot. The frustration will lead you to tense up and want to hit the ball a little harder, so you will swing a little faster—and your rhythm is gone.

Swinging faster doesn't make the ball go further.

Similarly, when you hit a great shot you must control the exhilaration. Otherwise, in the excitement you may walk a little faster which will make your heart beat a little faster, which will affect the timing of your swing—and again, your rhythm is gone.

Some evenings, as I reflect on the day that has just passed, I realize that I have spent the whole day in a rush. I look at what I achieved in the day, and often, I come to the realization that I really didn't need to rush. All the rushing didn't help.

A small example of this are my routine trips to Pittsburgh Airport. In the space of the year, I average more than one trip a week to the airport. From my home in south eastern Ohio to the airport is 32 miles. If I drive at the speed limit, which is fifty-five miles per hour, it will take me thirty-five minutes. If I drive at seventy miles per hour I risk getting a ticket, subject myself to the anxiety caused by the possibility of being pulled over, expose myself and my passengers to the danger of having an accident—and arrive at the airport in twenty-eight minutes. Imagine the anxiety I have been prepared to cause myself for the sake of arriving seven minutes earlier!

If the rhythm is going to be sacrificed in a certain situation, make sure it is a decision that you make, and not one that is forced upon you.

—⁓—

In this world that is always racing, we must learn to slow down. We must learn to create a pace for ourselves. We should learn to take control of—and maintain—the rhythm of our own lives.

I have always enjoyed walking. To me, it is a time to think about whatever is happening in my life. Recently, I have been trying to walk like a man who doesn't have a worry or care in the world. I begin walking as I have for years now, normally quite quickly, with thoughts chasing through my mind one after the other. As each issue arises I focus on it and decide whether or not I have done everything within my power regarding the matter. If I discover that I have, I surrender the situation. If I decide that I have not done everything that I should, I resolve to do so, and then surrender the situation. I then move on to the next issue and do the same with all the major issues in my life that day.

As the time I spend walking passes, I feel the burden of these various issues lifting from my shoulders, and I find myself slowing down to a nice, steady, peaceful pace. I begin walking to a rhythm. In that rhythm I find a peaceful heart, quiet mind, and restful spirit.

Learn to walk like a person who doesn't have a care in the world.

—⟿—

When we are in touch with *The Rhythm of Life* we are able to think about our lives as we live them, rather than as an after thought, or regret. It is good for the soul to live life reflectively.

Often on a golf course, as in life, you find yourself in places and situations you would rather not be in. In both golf and life you just have to work your way out of them as best you can. Golf is a thinking game—it's not about strength or stamina. Many people have the talent to hit great shots—but to do it consistently and often requires a certain mental fortitude and a psychological strength and focus. To be successful in the game of golf you must be a thinker. Nobody can focus their mind for five hours continually. The art of golf is to be able to focus your mind on the shot and relax your mind between shots. The same is true of life. Many people are gifted extraordinarily; very few use their gifts to the upper limits.

Upper limit achievement is the fruit of disciplined, selective, concentrated focus.

A life lived reflectively is a life lived effectively.

—⟿—

Slow down to find *The Rhythm of Life*. Maintain the rhythm in your life and enjoy the harmony it produces. Once you discover that peace deep within you, protect

it at all costs. For this peace alone is happiness, fulfillment, contentment, pleasure, and a sure sign that you
are evolving into a glorious being.

Reflection creates direction and inner peace. *The
Rhythm* of Life allows us to maintain that inner peace
even amidst the turmoil of the world.

————

I believe that God is Our Father. I believe He has wonderful plans for His children. Throughout history, no
sooner have our needs arisen than He has responded to
them. From the beginning, all He created He created in
harmony and with order. Since then His gifts have been
such that they help and encourage us to re-establish
and maintain this order in our lives. God's gifts give
rhythm to our lives. It is this rhythm, *The Rhythm of
Life*, that binds heaven and earth, man and nature, the
human and the Divine together in harmony, fulfilling
the words so often uttered *"your will be done on earth
as it is in heaven."*

Do you believe in the big bang theory? The idea that
all the beauty, wonder, and complexity of nature that
surrounds you, and is within you, is all the result of an
unintelligible explosion caused by a random mixture of
chemicals? No? Nor do I. Then why do we apply this
theory to our lives?

Perhaps, on the other hand, you believe that God created
the world, and the universe, and indeed all things, and that
He created them in an orderly fashion with harmony and
rhythm. Why don't we apply this truth to our lives?

Let us begin to live what we believe. Let us discover
The Rhythm of Life.

CHAPTER 5

CREATING THE RHYTHM

E ven now, two years beyond my crisis, it is still a daily challenge to maintain the rhythm in my own life. Some days I rise to the challenge, and when I do I am a better person. On other days, I fall into the same old traps. When I do, I try to learn from the experience so as to avoid those pitfalls in the future.

Finding the rhythm in our lives is difficult. In order to create *The Rhythm of Life* we must first confirm in our hearts and minds that the rhythm is desirable. Once we desire the rhythm we will use the daily activities of our lives to satisfy that desire. Desire is the greatest motivator.

In many ways our lives are a material expression of our desires. Desire is the seedling from which everything in our lives is born, good and bad, enriching and destructive.

The Rhythm of Life is desirable because it ensures our health and well-being—physically, emotionally, intellectually, and spiritually—by creating a lifestyle which fulfills our legitimate needs in each of these four areas.

The Rhythm of Life is desirable because it maximizes our efficiency and effectiveness in everything we do.

The Rhythm of Life is desirable because it lays the natural foundation for us to achieve our greatest dreams and achievements beyond what we have even dared to dream.

The Rhythm of Life is desirable because it leads to the satisfaction of the deepest desires of our hearts, which is the fulfillment of the will of God. The fruits of this alone are peace, joy, happiness, an increased ability to love, and an increased ability to be loved.

The Rhythm of Life is desirable.

If you can teach yourself, condition yourself, to desire those things which are good for you, there is nothing you cannot achieve or become. Desire is one of the greatest forces at work within the human being.

How do we condition ourselves to desire the things which are best for us? We desire the things we ponder. We desire the things we see every day.

Television is a perfect example. The combined audio-visual stimulus powerfully impacts us. We respond to the on-screen images with desire. What happens when you see something you like on television? You want it. In her book, *The Overspent American*, Juliet Schor describes a survey she conducted in 1998. Ms. Schor's research revealed that for every hour of television watched weekly, the consumers' spending rose by $208 a year.

We desire the things we ponder, the things we hold in our mind, and as such television is a form of pondering. Television drives consumer aspirations, not just the commercials, but the stylish clothing worn by actors and the affluent settings of many of the shows.

Great sporting champions ponder and desire victory. Great entrepreneurs ponder and desire financial wealth. Great saints ponder and desire intimacy with God.

If you begin to ponder the things that are good for you, you will begin to desire them. If you begin to desire them, you will soon begin to attain them.

THE THREE INSTRUMENTS

I wish to share with you *The Three Instruments* that allowed me to escape and recover from that tragic period in my life when I was so exhausted, overwhelmed, depressed, and confused.

My experience in Austria led me to anchor my life in these three simple instruments. *The First Instrument* involves regular sleep. *The Second Instrument* deals with regular prayer and reflection. *The Third Instrument* delves into the ancient tradition of the seventh day as a day of rest, reflection, and renewal.

These three instruments impact the very philosophical foundation of our lives, while at the same time being rooted in our day-to-day activities. They are not rules and regulations. They do not rob us of our individuality, but rather help us to discover who we truly are, and encourage us to become champions of selfhood.

The instruments shine the light of wisdom into the deep places of our hearts, minds, bodies, and spirits, revealing to us all of our strengths and weaknesses. They encourage us to look at the different areas of our lives and to examine different aspects of ourselves—to observe the ways we respond to certain events, activities, people, and circumstances.

From this we gain the self-knowledge we have spoken so much about. With this knowledge we are in a position to understand our own unique legitimate needs in each of the four areas—physical, emotional, intellectual, and spiritual.

The three instruments therefore lay the foundation for these needs to be met. The result is a man completely in harmony with his *self*, a woman completely in harmony with her *self*. This harmony produced by *The Rhythm of Life* increases our effectiveness in our work; makes us more present in our relationships; and empowers us with a spiritual presence and focus—all of which gives birth to that deep and abiding peace, an inexpressible joy and satisfaction, and a sense of fulfillment which burns within us, igniting an excitement and passion for life.

GET OUT OF BED

Your aims and aspirations may reside in the upper realms of the intellectual life. Your dreams and goals may dwell higher than the highest peaks of this world in the spiritual realm. But no matter how high, noble, and spiritual your aspirations may be, you must build them on natural foundations. In the human being that foundation consists firstly of physical well-being.

Have you ever been unemployed? Have you ever lived with someone who was unemployed? What happens? What changes? Most people suffer from an acute blow to their self-esteem which produces depression in one form or another. A classic symptom of this depression is when they don't have to get out of bed—they don't. Often when people lose their job, they tend to slip into the habit of sleeping in. After a while they only shave every second day, then every third day. When they do get out of bed, they go down to the local store to get the newspaper and look for available positions. But by the time they call about the jobs it is early afternoon—maybe late afternoon—and the positions are already filled. Before you know it, they only shave when they have a job interview, which is almost never, because they don't get out of bed early enough to make the calls in time.

They fall into a rhythm of life. A certain rhythm which grabs a hold of them and takes them for a ride. We call that ride "a vicious cycle." Where does it take them? NOWHERE.

This rhythm of life does not energize them or bring the best out of them, but rather drains them of their energy and prevents them from achieving anything worthwhile. This rhythm of life that has kidnapped them does not support the fulfillment of their legitimate needs physically, emotionally, intellectually, or spiritually. This rhythm of life they have adopted is self-destructive.

That vicious cycle exists in one way or another in each and every one of our lives. We get caught up in certain patterns of behavior which are self-destructive, a rhythm of life which does not attend to our legitimate needs, a lifestyle which does not enrich and fulfill us.

Is your lifestyle destroying you?

How do we escape these vicious cycles? Little by little. Small victories are the key. If you decide to become a marathon runner you don't go out and try to run a marathon straight away. You start by running one mile a day, then two, three, five, and seven. Over time you build yourself up, and as you strengthen and develop, you extend the distances. Many victories are won before a marathon runner's first race.

Can you do one hundred sit-ups? If you are not in the habit of doing sit-ups regularly, you probably think it is impossible to do one hundred sit-ups consecutively right now. But if you start today by doing twenty each day for a week, then thirty a day for a week, and so on, before too long you will be able to do a hundred sit-ups—and the impossible will have been made possible. That is the greatness of the human spirit—making the unknown known, making the impossible possible. Small victories, one upon another, are the making of every great champion.

These small victories build strength and confidence. The victory over twenty sit-ups builds strength, courage, and confidence to achieve the victory of doing thirty sit-ups the following week. If, on the other hand, you tried to do one hundred sit-ups every day, the first day you might stop after eighteen, the second day after twenty-one, the third day after twenty-five, the fourth day after twenty-six. After a week, most people would become so discouraged from failing over and over again, they would quit.

Set goals that stretch you but do not break you.

In the way that these small victories build strength, confidence, and courage in athletes, they can do the same for us in every area of our lives whether in our professional work, our relationships, or our spiritual practices.

A large part of success in anything is victory. Success is mostly about victory over ourselves. The habitual and repetitious achievement of such victories produces the quality of self-discipline in a person's character. This self-discipline is the founding ideal of all great nations and religions in history. It is the founding father of freedom, and the foundation of the nation, culture, and dream we call America.

If you give your body a choice, it will always take the easy way out. Your body lies. It tells you it cannot when it can.

How did Michael Johnson become the fastest man in the world? By running when he felt like running? No. Michael Johnson tells his body what it is and is not allowed to feel, and when it is and is not allowed to feel those things. His success comes from his mastery of his body. His higher faculties—intellect, will, spirit—reign over his lower faculties—bodily instincts. Each time his body says, "I can't" he pushes it a little further. The body has a natural capacity to increase its strength and abilities. The heart, mind, and spirit are all equipped with the same natural capacity.

Does Martina Hingis or Patrick Rafter hit tennis balls only when they feel like it? Did Bill Gates achieve what he has by sleeping in until one o'clock in the afternoon? Does Emmett Smith only show up to practice when he is in the mood for it? Did Abraham Lincoln only do the things he felt like doing? Do you think Mother Teresa always felt like taking care of the poorest of the poor?

One thing is certain. If you only ever do what you feel like doing, your life will be miserable and you will be a failure.

—⁓—

Victory over self leads to ever increasing levels of achievement in any field. Our first opportunity for victory each day is when the alarm clock goes off and it is time to get out of bed. This is the first victory of the day. Most people when they wake up would prefer to lay in bed a little longer. The body cries out, "just ten more minutes." Who is the master? Your lower faculties— bodily instincts, or your higher faculties—intellect, will, spirit? Do you do what your body tells you to do, or does your body do what you tell it to do?

If your dreams, goals, and purpose are not enough to inspire you to want to get out of bed in the morning, then you need to re-think your dreams, goals, and purpose.

Get out of bed. Grasp the day from the first moment. Achieve that first victory. Look at it as a victory. Affirm it as a victory. Victory encourages the human spirit to soar higher. Small victories are the mentors of greater victories. The human spirit responds to victory. Victory elevates the human spirit. We must learn to find victory in everything, even in defeat.

The First Instrument

The First Instrument for creating *The Rhythm of Life* is to *Get Out of Bed*. It sounds deceptively simple. In Chapter Two we began our investigation of legitimate physical need with a brief discussion of our need for food. If we do not eat we will die. We have a legitimate need to eat and to drink. Our legitimate needs are those activities and things that allow us to maximize our health and well-being. These needs are an intended part of the Divine plan. Sleep is also one of our legitimate physical needs. If you do not sleep, over time you will become delusional, and finally over an extended period of time, sleep deprivation will lead to insanity. If you were forced to stay awake long enough, you would of course die.

Over the past twenty years, the study of sleep has grown considerably in popularity. These studies have sought to discover when we should sleep, for how long we should sleep, where we should sleep, and how we should sleep—in order to maintain optimum health and well-being.

In order to apply *The First Instrument* to our lives we must first ask these questions of ourselves. When do I sleep? For how long do I sleep? Where do I sleep? How do I sleep? But firstly, we must ask the question philosophers, scientists, and children have been asking since the dawn of human history: Why? Why do we sleep?

The common answer to this question is, "We sleep because we have to sleep." It is true, we must sleep. Sleep is essential for survival. However, this answer only displays an attitude towards sleep. It does not answer the question.

We sleep in order to be renewed. Sleep refreshes us. Sleep energizes us. Our sleep not only brings rest, renewal, and energy to our bodies, but also to our hearts, minds, and spirits. When we view it from this very positive perspective, and consciously approach it with these things in mind, we maximize the effects of sleep.

Conscious living maximizes the enrichment of every activity and experience in our lives.

Conscious living simply means knowing what you are doing while you are doing it.

When we approach sleep as something we must do, or as a burden and limitation, we reduce the refreshing, renewing, and energizing effects sleep has upon our bodies, hearts, minds, and spirits.

For a few moments now, pause and reflect upon your attitude towards sleep. You will gain very little from this discussion unless you take this important step, and are therefore able to ask yourself the other questions: when, where, and how do I sleep? Many of us will not be able to answer these right away. In order to do so, we must seek this very important self-knowledge.

—–⁓⁓⁓—

I believe the most important issue regarding sleep is when you sleep. Why do so many people feel they don't get enough sleep? People of all different sleeping habits seem to want more. The issue here is not the quantity of our sleep, but rather, the quality of our sleep.

You may think sleep is sleep. Yet, numerous studies have revealed that people who sleep at the same time every night are considerably healthier than those who do not. They are affected by common colds less than one-third as many times as people who do not sleep at regular hours. The incidence of depression is also significantly lower with people who sleep at r-egular hours.

In order to implement *The First Instrument* in our lives, in order to be able to *Get Out of Bed* refreshed and energized in the morning, there is some prepara-tion to be done. Once again, this preparation involves self-knowledge. If you know you need to get out of bed at 7am in order to get ready for your day in a calm and peaceful manner, and if you also know that if you don't get seven hours sleep you become grouchy and miserable, then be fair to yourself. Be kind to yourself, and use your self-knowledge. It is powerful to live by what you know about yourself. Make sure that by midnight you are in bed, despite what problems emerge—schedules, stresses, social situations, and poor habits. Often these are what hinder our ability to get the sleep we need.

For example, in order to be in bed and asleep at midnight every night, you will certainly find yourself leaving some social events early. The question is, for the sake of a couple of extra hours at a party, are you prepared to throw your life into chaos?

Yes, there are exceptions. No, you do not have to be in bed every night by midnight for the rest of your life. But, in our lives the exception has become the rule. There is no consistency to our sleeping patterns and that is costing us dearly—physically, emotionally, intellectually, and spiritually.

Many of us have been falsely led to believe that sleep is an expendable element, and that it can be used defensively. Sleep should be used offensively, not defensively. Sleep builds us up. Sleep is one of the indispensable natural elements of our lives. Sleep is one of our legitimate needs. Sleep is intended to make us stronger, more vibrant, productive, loving, and alert individuals. Sleep is important and should be given priority.

Our modern world works against this in so many ways. For instance, a great number of people uphold lack of sleep as a source of pride. Some people believe that excessive dedication to waking hours overrules the necessity for rest and regular sleep. They convince themselves that in order to be successful in their chosen field they must sacrifice sleep and rest—they even believe this to be heroic. These ideas are particularly common in business. Perhaps they need to return to the text books and reconsider the concept of "long term residual effect," and ponder it in relation to their own lives.

We have no greater evidence of the importance of sleep than in the habits of those who are highly successful. Recently, I had the opportunity to meet Olympian Alberto Salazar after one of my talks in Oregon. He had a presence, the presence of a champion, a certain strength, and yet a profound humility.

Do you suppose when Alberto Salazar won the gold medal for the Marathon at the 1992 Olympic games, he credited his success to sleeping less than all of the other athletes in his field? No, Salazar trained harder, rested more effectively, was more attuned to his dietary needs, was more in touch with his desire to win—and has been leaving parties early for years because he knows he has to get up early the next morning to train. If he doesn't train well he won't compete well.

The truth is, people are walking around half asleep all the time. Everyday, people are exhausted. They are fatigued. Fatigue has become a pattern in our lives. This is a sad testament to how little we observe, know, and respect ourselves.

When was the last time you woke up and felt renewed, refreshed, and excited to get into your day? That is what I want you to experience, not occasionally—but everyday.

On the other hand, do you remember the last time you had to get up early after a late night? How did you feel? Did you say to yourself, "I wish I didn't have to get out of bed this morning"? Or perhaps, "I am never going to stay out late again on a work night." How was your day? Were you a picture of energy? Did you enjoy the day? Were you efficient? Effective? Happy?

The real question is, will you let it happen again? Each of us should know how much sleep we require in order to function at maximum efficiency—be it six, seven, or eight hours. When will we begin to use this valuable information to our own advantage?

In this era of lust, we lust even after knowledge. Foolishly we believe that wisdom is the amassing of knowledge. We want to know more, but we do not want to live what we already know.

—*w*—

The first step is to sleep at the same time every night. In order to attune ourselves to *The Rhythm of Life*, we must adopt a regular pattern of sleep—going to bed at the same time and getting up at the same time. It really is quite simple, and yet, on occasions when I have verbally shared this idea with people, they have looked at me as if I was asking the impossible. It is perhaps testament to how complex and cluttered our lives have become. It is perhaps testament to how out of control our lives are. Begin to take control of your life—adopt a regular sleeping schedule.

This is the most basic way I know to create *The Rhythm of Life* and it is the essence of The First Instrument. It brings a consistency to the general structure and organization of our lives. In the area of physical well-being, it is the first step towards maximizing our energy, and therefore the first step towards increasing our effectiveness in everything we do.

I have seen it work in my own life and I have seen it work in the lives of others. If you go to bed and get up at the same time everyday, weekdays and weekends, in less than ten days you will feel like a different person. New energy, new enthusiasm, new passion for life.

It will be a challenge. It will be difficult at times. It will cost. It is simply a matter of priorities. This regular sleeping schedule will empower you to give your best to everything you do everyday. You will no longer find yourself saying, "I just want to get through today and get home to bed!" That is no way to live. Everyday should be savored. Being rested is not just about being awake—it's about being able to completely devote yourself to whatever is before you in every single moment of the day. It is about living life to the fullest.

It is also important that you give consideration to how long you sleep. The secret with sleep is the same wisdom that applies to just about everything that affects the body—guard against extremes. Too little sleep is not good for us, and too much sleep is not good for us. If we sleep too little we wake up fatigued, and if we sleep too much we wake up fatigued. Test different sleeping times for several days. Grow to know yourself, and what amount of sleep allows you to function most effectively.

Consideration should also be given to where you sleep and the environment you sleep in. Once again, try different things and get to know yourself. If it is too hot or too cold, how does that affect the effectiveness of your sleep?

How you sleep can also make a radical difference—whether on your stomach, on your side, or on your back. Observe yourself. Know yourself. Use the knowledge you gain about yourself to live a happier, healthier, fuller life.

When I was eighteen and first in college under the spell of the "modern lie" I used to believe that eating and sleeping were a waste of time. Twenty minutes was the absolute maximum I would dedicate to sitting at table for a meal, and mostly I ate on the run. When it came to sleep—two, three, four hours a night, and some nights I would not go to bed at all. Over the past seven years I have learned a lot about myself and I know now that without seven hours of sleep each night, I am no good to anyone.

It is time we began to see sleep not as a limitation or burden, but as a gift. Embrace this gift. Treasure the gift. Cherish the gift. Enjoy the gift. Use the gift of sleep to its maximum advantage. Use sleep to begin to create *The Rhythm of Life*.

THE SACRED HOUR

Image or light, that is the question. We tend to spend our lives dedicated to the image, to the material. The image represents the body. The light represents the spirit.

Do you identify more with your body or with your spirit? The highest levels of living are experienced when we have an absolute disregard for the body beyond our basic needs, and a complete adherence to the promptings of the Divine Spirit within us. It is then that we form our identity from the spirit within, when we let the sweet light within us shine.

Most of us, however, are dedicated to the body, to the image. We see and value ourselves not in terms of the spirit, but in relation to the body. We find our identity through the body. We form, and live by, an image made up of physical and sensory perception.

Do you find your identity through your body or through your spirit? Are you dedicated to the image or to the light? The image is an illusion. The light is truth.

If you are uncertain as to which you are dedicated, try any or all of these three exercises. Firstly, try to sit completely still in a silent room for an extended period of time. Completely still. No movement whatsoever, except that which is necessary to breathe. Secondly, in the cool of the evening, sit outside on your porch with only light clothing on, and in a very short period, you will most likely discover that you are dedicated to the body and the image. Finally, eat nothing but bread and drink nothing but water for twenty-four hours. How easy or difficult are these things for you?

A person who is completely dedicated to the light is capable of anything.

Prayer shifts our dedication from the image to the light.

—⁓—

We live in an age that is obsessed and preoccupied with the material. We live in a time dominated by greed and lust. We live in the era of perpetual noise and motion; an age obsessed with speed. These are the characteristics of our times. These are the trends, mindsets, and structures that distract and prevent us from discovering *The Rhythm of Life*. And yet, this is the world we must live in.

I want to live in peace. This is my single greatest desire. Perhaps it sounds simplistic, but when I have this peace I am happy and in love with life. Without this peace, life is a drudgery. I have experienced this peace. It is real. It is the most intense pleasure life has to offer. It heightens the sensitivity of all the senses and increases the intensity of all of life's other pleasures. It is both calm and exhilarating. It could be likened to taking a journey to the deepest places and the highest places all at once. It is a contradiction and yet perfectly in balance. It is the fruit of an intimate harmony between the physical, emotional, intellectual, and spiritual elements of the human person.

Peace is not the absence of pain or pressure. Nor is it the absence of activity. Peace is not laying on a beach without a worry in the world. Peace is not born by doing nothing.

This peace I speak of, is a certainty in my heart and mind that I am using my life for a worthy purpose—that each day I am able to love more than the day before, that I am becoming a better person each day, that in my own way I am touching and improving the lives of others. It is maintained with the conviction that the way I am spending the energies of my life makes sense.

—⁓—

A few months ago I spent a couple of days with a very wealthy gentleman in Europe, a friend of a friend. This man has more money than you and I could physically count in a lifetime. All his life he has worked very hard and his achievements in business are admirable. One morning at breakfast it was just the two of us and he began to speak. "There is something different about you Matthew. I don't know what it is, but it is special and rare. You make me ponder life." I said nothing and he said nothing for several minutes. Then he continued, "I will tell you this because you are young and perhaps it will be of some use to you. I am a very wealthy man. I have more houses than ten families could live in, more boats and cars than I could ever use, more money than I could ever spend. Everywhere I go I am treated like royalty... but, I have no peace. Peace... and the funny thing is, I would give everything I have, the things I have spent my whole life building, for just a little peace. As a little boy I had it, but now as an old man, I have no peace." The most overwhelming sorrow and pity for this man welled up inside me, and I wondered how many others felt this way. I couldn't help but think to myself, "It's not a 'funny thing,' it's a tragedy."

As time goes by, what I discover most about people is that we want to live in peace.

This is why in a time when so many people are turning their backs on prayer, I am trying to embrace prayer with my whole being. Prayer gives me that peace. Prayer teaches me to use my life for a worthy purpose. Prayer reveals that purpose. Prayer warns me when I wander from the narrow path. Prayer increases my ability to love and my ability to be loved. Prayer fills me with hope, and that hope is not the conviction that everything will turn out well, but rather the certainty that the way I am spending my life makes sense regardless of how it turns out. Prayer allows me to live my life in peace.

If you look into the eyes of the people you meet today, you will see clouds and storms, fear and doubt, confusion and worry, anxiety and restlessness. But very rarely, in this day and age that has turned its back on prayer, do you look into a person's eyes and see the calm, still, peaceful waters of a crystal clear lake.

—⚬⚬⚬—

Prayer is essential. Prayer cuts through and clarifies. Prayer reminds us of what is really important. Prayer awakens our awareness to our legitimate needs. Prayer is the great friend who introduces us to ourselves. Prayer is the great mediator that introduces us to God. Prayer is the faithful friend who points out who we are and who we are capable of being. Prayer reveals the deepest desires of our hearts and points out the path that was ordained for us from the beginning of time. Prayer whispers those golden words, "That is your star, go now and follow it." Prayer gifts us with purpose and direction, and peace in that direction. Prayer is a journey and a destination. Prayer is a chance to become intimately familiar with the better person we know we can be—and that familiarity is the beginning of wisdom. Prayer helps. Prayer is important. Prayer is needed. We need prayer. Prayer doesn't need us, and God doesn't need prayer. Prayer doesn't help God, it helps us. It isn't something we must do, it is something we should do. I pray because I cannot help it. I pray because in every moment the need flows out of me. I pray because I am a better person when I do.

Pray.

The Second Instrument

The Second Instrument I used to rediscover *The Rhythm of Life* I call *The Sacred Hour*. Essentially, it consists of an hour of prayer, but not necessarily in the way you may presently conceive an hour of prayer to be. If you are not presently in the habit of praying, the idea of praying for an hour may seem frightening or even impossible. Be open. Open your heart and your mind to a new understanding of prayer.

The purpose of prayer is to help you make the journey from *Point A* to *Point B*, and to become the better person you know you can be, which indeed, is the purpose of life. The common mistake is to think of prayer as easy. I assure you, prayer is the most difficult thing in the world to do. In prayer we find ourselves standing on the edge of a deep, dark, abyss—the world of the Divine, Infinite, and Eternal. In prayer we come face to face with ourselves and face to face with God, and at different times both of these encounters can be very frightening. Prayer is difficult. But, those who learn to master prayer come to master themselves, and those who come to master themselves become the instruments of tremendous good and are able to master every other human activity.

In my life I believe that everything good comes from knowing and living in the will of God. I believe that I was created for a purpose. I believe that there is a plan for each of us—a Divine blueprint—a mission. That plan perfectly intertwines our talents, our legitimate needs, and our deepest desires—to bring about this perfect harmony between body, heart, mind, and spirit. In following that plan I believe we find peace and prosperity, freedom and fulfillment.

We may, of course, reject this plan, this blueprint, this mission. And there lies the mystery of freedom and love.

The will of God is the perfection of the creature. The will of God is that you make the journey from *Point A* to *Point B*. Each step along that path forms an allegiance and bond with the will of God. It is in this journey that we discover the glory of life. It is in prayer that we discover the glory of God. And, it is by living what we discover in prayer that we become the glory of God. The will of God is that you become the better person you know you can be. Your unique and individual personality, talents, needs, and desires is what makes your journey different from mine. All of these are unveiled in the classroom of silence.

Prayer is the great *classroom of silence*. During my travels over the past five years I have continually heard people whisper, "How did he become so wise at such a young age?" Wisdom is not a mass of accumulated knowledge. Wisdom is those little pieces of knowledge that have the power to change our lives. Wisdom is truth lived. Wisdom is the fruit of a reflective heart. Wisdom is the fruit of silence.

When I was nineteen God touched my life in a very special way. It was at that time, leading up to when I first began speaking, that I began to seriously pray—and that I felt God inviting me into the classroom of silence. For almost six months every day I would sit alone in silence, pondering and reflecting upon my life, the world, Christ, and the Gospels for three, four, five, sometimes six hours a day.

It is from this experience that I believe, and have written things such as, *"You can learn more in an hour of silence than you can in a year from books,"* and *"Noise is the mouthpiece of the world. Silence is the mouthpiece of God. It is in the classroom of silence that God bestows his infinite wisdom on men and women."*

We live in a noisy world. People wake up to clock radios, listen to the news while they shower, watch television while they eat breakfast, get into the car and listen to the morning shows on the way to work, listen to music all day over the intercom, talk incessantly on the phone between any number of meetings ...We need to stop the noise.

Everything great in history has arisen from silence. Even great noise. Beethoven and Mozart closed themselves off from the world and inhabited silent rooms for days at a time in order to hear things that no one else could hear—sounds so glorious that they themselves would never hear in the midst of the world, and yet, sounds that the world would never know if Beethoven and Mozart had not befriended silence.

USA Today conducted a survey last year in which people were asked to name the ten things they feared the most. The most feared was death. After death, flying. After flying, silence—closely followed by public speaking, dogs, snakes and spiders. Why do we fear silence? Why do we avoid silence?

Silence introduces us to ourselves—for better and for worse. Silence convicts, suggests, and challenges— yes. But silence also consoles, heals, comforts, clears the mind, and gives courage to the weary heart. Peace is the fruit of silence.

Why do we fear and avoid silence? The truth is, most people believe that everything within them is worthless and embarrassing. That is why we live in a world terrified of silence and full of people dedicated to imitating other people instead of developing the unique individual that they are themselves.

Befriend silence. I am not suggesting that you spend four, five, six hours a day in silence. Take ten minutes a day in your church, or in a quiet chair at home. Leave the radio off in the car on the way to work, have a television free evening once a week in the home. Try it. It works.

I close my eyes so that I may see things that I could never see with my eyes open, things that would never come to be if I did not close my eyes. I enter the classroom of silence to listen, and there I hear things I would never hear in this noisy world, the murmurings of my heart and soul that lead me to my future.

———

What are you prepared to do to significantly increase the level of peace, happiness, and fulfillment in your life? How far are you prepared to go? How much are you prepared to give? Are you prepared to give one hour a day?

I would like to encourage you to set aside one hour a day. This time becomes another landmark in our day and helps us to restore and maintain *The Rhythm of Life*. It's difficult to set aside one hour a day, I know, but I'm going to try and convince you that it is worth making the effort and initial sacrifice.

For this one hour I want you to pray. I do not want you to go into your church and mindlessly repeat prayers that you were taught as a child until you either fall asleep, or are bored out of your brain. I would like you to discover the joy of prayer. I want this time to be a joy for you.

If prayer was something you loved and longed for, you would have no difficulty spending one hour a day in prayer. The secret to prayer is discovering ways to make it something you love and long for, something you know and are comfortable with.

After all, we love the people, activities, and things we are familiar with. We love what we know.

———◦◦◦———

There are hundreds of ways to pray and in time you will discover which ways work best for you. My intention here is merely to share some ideas with you, to construct a collage from some of my own personal experiences of prayer in the hope that they may be helpful and insightful to you.

Sometimes my heart is tormented by restlessness and anxiety. Sometimes my mind is distracted by a hundred little problems. Sometimes my spirit is burdened and I feel the weight of the world upon my shoulders. At these times, prayer allows me to put into words exactly what is troubling me. I sit down in a quiet place, close my eyes, and in a gentle mental dialogue I tell God what is on my heart and mind. I explain what is bothering me. I explain the situation. I tell him how I feel and why I feel that way. When I am finished I sit there in silence and listen. Usually, by the time I am finished explaining, I know what it is I need to do.

It is often at these times that I find myself wandering into a church and sitting quietly in the presence of God.

Most of us know what we should and need to do. But that knowledge gets buried beneath the messages of the world and the opinions of family and friends. Sometimes we just need someone to talk to, or someone to listen to us. How often do we begin to talk to someone about a problem, and before we are finished explaining the situation to that person, we see things much more clearly in our own mind, and we know what we should do? God is the great listener.

—⁓⁓—

Some days I am so distracted by the happenings of the day that I am simply unable to concentrate enough to engage in this dialogue. On those days I like to use some reading material to bring me into focus, to help me concentrate.

I am fascinated with the life of Jesus—a leader who for Himself wanted nothing, which in itself is a great sign of sincerity and honesty. I am fascinated with the Gospels which tell us of His life and teachings. They are so simple, and yet, deeply profound and potent. Very often I use the life of Jesus in the Gospels during this *Sacred Hour*. Slowly, deliberately, reflectively I read over a short passage. Once, twice, three times—trying to delve into and extract some of the mystery and wisdom.

Reading can be a very powerful tool to bring us into focus during prayer. Read slowly, savor the words, ponder what they mean to you in your particular circumstances. There are hundreds of books that would serve as good companions for *The Sacred Hour*.

—⁓⁓—

On other days when I find myself entering *The Sacred Hour* restless and anxious, I use the meditation of the red rose which I have spoken of so often in my talks and seminars.

I begin by sitting down in a quiet place, sitting comfortably, sitting still, and closing my eyes. Then, in my mind's eye, I envision before me a single red rose. In the Middle Ages, the single red rose was a symbol of Christ. If you travel through Europe you will often find this image in the stained-glass windows of the great cathedrals. You will also find it was used to decorate many of the manuscripts of that period. For you it could be any image that leads you to focus your attention on God and the perfection you seek.

With my attention now focused on the rose, I slowly allow all other thoughts to flow out of my mind. Distractions are inevitable. When I realize that a thought or idea has reentered my mind, as soon as I am aware that I have been taken hostage by a distraction, I free my mind once again by returning to the single red rose in my mind's eye.

Over a few minutes my mind is able to still, and my heart and soul begin to heighten in awareness. I find myself in the presence of God. Some days my whole time of prayer can consist of this exercise of stillness and focus. It is one of my favorite ways to spend my time on planes. On most days I use this meditation for a few minutes to begin my prayer before moving on to one of the other forms of prayer we have discussed.

We must learn to turn from the outer life of noise and confusion, towards the inner life of silence and serenity.

—◦◦◦—

One of the classic counsels from the Bible is, *"Be still and know that I am God."* The stillness is important. In this stillness we are able to contemplate the things of the spirit. The stillness frees us from the limitations of the body and sets the spirit free to soar. The spirit within us is fearless. The spirit within us does not doubt, it knows.

In the stillness we form a connection with the spirit within. Through this practice, over time, we come to perceive ourselves as a spiritual being having a physical experience, rather than just a physical being.

In discussing the rose meditation I mentioned that I would sit still. When I say still, I mean completely still. No movement whatsoever, not even a fraction of an inch. The only movement is the gentle rising of my chest as I breathe.

Sit up straight, but not forced. Erect, but relaxed. Place both feet flat on the ground spaced comfortably apart. Rest your hands in your lap. And now, sit still. Completely still.

Let me warn you, if you try to practice this method of prayer there are some common traps. Within thirty seconds of making yourself comfortable, and resolving to be still, your body will object and inform you that it is uncomfortable. Thirty seconds ago you were reasonably comfortable. A more comfortable position is only an illusion. If you move to find a more comfortable position, you will spend your entire time of prayer shifting and moving—approximately every thirty seconds—and once again the body will have triumphed.

If you are able to ignore the temptation to search for the position which is perfectly comfortable, you will overcome the first obstacle, inform the body who is master, and move to a deeper level.

Your next hurdle will come within two minutes. You will have an itch. Perhaps on your hand, your neck, your nose, or just under your eye. Your body will beckon you to scratch the itch. To do so you will have to move, which will break the dominance of mind and spirit over body. Don't. Acknowledge the itch and ask yourself: Is it bearable? Will it kill me to ignore it? Of course it is bearable, and it certainly will not kill you. Stay still. Ignore it. Once you resolve not to respond to the call of the body, the itch will increase in intensity for a few moments. Then as your resolve not to respond builds, the itch will fade. Throughout this, you will be progressing to new levels of stillness, silence, solitude—all leading you to oneness with the Spirit within.

Another danger is that as we become silent and still, our minds clear. The calm produces clarity of thought. You will be reminded of things you had forgotten, things you need to do. All of these are temptations to stop.

For me, I find that as soon as I come into the stillness and silence, this calm produces all types of writing ideas. My temptation is to stop praying and to write. But I find, if I ignore those initial temptations I am led to even deeper ideas later in my prayer.

These temptations will re-emerge occasionally—itches, discomfort, distractions, the temptation to stop, to scratch, the temptation to shuffle into a more comfortable position. I tell myself—it won't kill me, and I ignore it. It irritates for a few moments, sometimes minutes, but then it goes away and with that victory we are taken to even higher places of contemplation.

It is in those places that I have experienced the most glorious moments of my life. The experience cannot be described, but if you are able to taste it for a moment, just once, you will long and yearn for that everyday—and then prayer will become your passion and pleasure. You will go to the classroom of silence everyday for peace and guidance, to discover who you are, and to summon the strength to be true to your *self*. Only then will the words I have placed on the pages of this book take on their full meaning for you and your life. You will re-read these lines and discover layer upon layer of meaning.

You are about to discover how difficult it is to sit still. If you persevere you will discover the unfathomable power of stillness and silence. Only in this state, I believe, can we come to truly know the deepest needs and desires of our being.

Prayer is a contraction. In prayer we close ourselves off from the world, from people, places, and possessions, we abandon the seduction of noise, and close our eyes. But from these contractions are born the most remarkable expansions, and we are empowered by the Divine Spirit to see things before unseen, to hear things before unheard, and to become an unimagined creation.

Prayer is a contraction which produces an expansion.

Be still and know that I am God. Be still and know that I am. Be still and know. Be still. Be.

―――

There are days when I like to spend *The Sacred Hour* taking a long walk in a quiet place. I like to walk slowly making sure not to lose my breath. I like to try to walk like a man who hasn't a care in the world, practicing the exercise I described in Chapter Four.

It is amazing the difference the way you breathe can make. For example, if you are in a pressure situation, or you are frustrated, how are you breathing? Heavily and quickly—short breaths. Now, concentrate on your breathing. Breathe slowly and deeply. Within minutes your whole demeanor can be changed and controlled.

Another example: You get into the shower and the water turns freezing cold. You are stunned. Your reaction is to gasp at short breaths of air. Breathe deeply and you will be able to tolerate the cold water.

How you breathe during prayer is important. When you first begin your prayer, pay attention to your breathing. Breathe slowly and deeply. This will help you to calm down, relax, and surrender to the peacefulness of prayer.

We eliminate stress and invite relaxation by returning our focus to the basics of life. There is nothing more fundamental than breathing.

Breathe. Don't forget to breathe. The way you breathe can change your state more quickly than any other controllable physiological aspect of the human person.

—∿∿—

On other days, particularly when I am visiting my family and friends in Australia, I like to spend my *Sacred Hour* sitting on a quiet beach, listening to the waves roll in and out. The rhythm of the waves has a calming, soothing quality. There is a sacred connection between God and nature. It is mysterious, but real.

When I was a child my parents often took my brothers and me to the beach. We would swim and build sand castles. We used to go to Manly Beach. I always go there when I return to Sydney. There is something powerful and wonderful about the places of our childhood. In a mystical way they remind us of who we once were, which brings into focus who we are now. They remind us of our story. Everyone has one, and our own individual story is an indispensable tool in the journey to grow and change. I like to visit Manly Beach, to eat in restaurants where my family ate on special occasions, to walk on the soccer fields I once played on.

Visit the places of your childhood. That would be a *Sacred Hour* well spent.

———

Prayer is a time to share our joys and troubles with God, but it is so much more than just that. Prayer is a time to dream and visualize.

There is one thing my golf coach told me that I have never forgotten. He used to say, *"If you cannot see the shot, you cannot hit the shot. Stand behind the ball. Look at the ball, then look at the hole. Visualize the shot you want to hit. If you cannot see the shot, you cannot hit the shot."*

It is true for just about everything. Van Gough was able to stand before an empty canvas, unlock his imagination and see something that wasn't there. Thomas Edison was able to see things that didn't even exist— yet. Martin Luther King was able to see something that wasn't before him, but that he knew should be.

Van Gough once wrote, *"The thing has already taken form in my mind before I start. The first attempts are absolutely unbearable. I say this because I want you to know that if you see something worthwhile in what I am doing, it is not by accident but because of real direction and purpose."*

The first attempts at prayer are also often unbearable.

This principle of visualization is also true for our most important work in this life. If you cannot see the better person you know you can be, you cannot be that better person. Prayer is the place and time to visualize the ways in which you can become the better person. Prayer is an opportunity to join your heart and mind to the heart and mind of God and to visualize everything you dream, hope, and wish to achieve, and everything you long to be. Here lies the power of prayer. Make no mistake, prayer unleashes the unfathomable potential of the human spirit—the power to visualize and engage unrealized potential.

Would the same idea work for a young man who wanted to become the greatest basketball player in history? Michael Jordan once said, *"I visualized where I wanted to be, what kind of player I wanted to become. I knew exactly where I wanted to go, and I focused on getting there."*

—ɷ—

It is also by prayer that God empowers us to overcome faults, addictions, and vices. For example, suppose there is someone who really annoys you at school or at work. Over and over the same situation arises and you become frustrated, annoyed, even angered. That one situation, and others like it, can destroy your peace for a whole day, even for days at a time.

Do not let that person rob you of your peace. Imagine the situation. Visualize it as it has happened before. Now, imagine the perfect way to respond in that situation in order to remain calm and peaceful. How long does it take to visualize that response? Ten seconds. In the empty moments of the day, between tasks, while you are walking from one place to another, imagine that situation. Visualize it, over and over again. Visualize your response, your perfect response, over and over again. Imagine yourself remaining calm and peaceful in that situation. Visualize yourself responding to that situation perfectly twenty times a day. It will cost you less than three and a half minutes a day, and within two weeks I promise you will be responding in exactly the same way you have visualized.

Thought determines action. Do not let your whole life be a reaction to the things that happen around you each day. Let your life be an action.

—⁓—

The Sacred Hour is a time of renewal and refreshment. It is a time of spiritual nourishment. It is a time to slow down and remind ourselves of what is really important. *The Sacred Hour* is an opportunity to bring focus and direction to our lives. A time to dream and visualize. And yet, our prayer should not be confined to this one hour each day.

At the end of my *Sacred Hour* each day I feel peaceful. I feel confident I can handle the events and situations that are before me. But after five minutes back into the hustle and bustle of daily life, it is so easy to lose that peace and focus.

I try to sustain the effect of the *Sacred Hour* by using a simple and ancient spiritual technique. I repeat to myself a simple phrase, or word over and over again, hundreds of times throughout the day. This technique is known as a mantra and has been used for centuries in several different religious traditions. The phrase I like to use is the first line of a prayer attributed to Francis of Assisi, *"Lord, make me an instrument of your peace."*

Throughout the day in those empty moments between tasks, in those minutes driving from one place to another, at times of frustration, pressure, anger, disappointment—I repeat this phrase over and over again. Slowly. Thoughtfully. I Allow it to reach down to the depths of my being.

After a while it becomes second nature to respond to certain situations internally first before responding externally. To reflect rather than speak or shout.

Try it. Find your own phrase. A quote, a word, a sentence that has the power to bring everything back into perspective for you. You will discover that there are so many gaps in the day, empty moments that can be used to refocus ourselves on what is really important.

The mantra has been a valuable tool for great spiritual leaders for hundreds of years. Successful people remind themselves of their goal in every waking moment of every hour of every day. Whether you seek to be a successful football player or successful in the spiritual life, the same principle applies. The mantra is a tool that will serve you to help stay focused—to keep your heart and mind fixed on your goal in every moment of every day.

—◈—

Sometimes life shakes us up a little. We become disoriented, overwhelmed, consumed by the day-to-day happenings of our lives. The British Navy has a practice known as an "All Still." When something goes wrong on a ship, particularly a submarine, the captain announces an "All Still." For three minutes no one is allowed to move or speak.

Our lives are an expression of what is within us. Life is an overflow of the heart. If within you are confused, frustrated, and exhausted, your actions will tell the same story.

Three minutes of silence and stillness can have an exponential effect in the middle of a turbulent situation. In my own life I have found that between meetings, phone calls, or in the middle of a group project, an "All Still" can make all the difference. It is an opportunity to catch your breath and put things in perspective.

———

Prayer contributes to the health and well-being of the whole person. Studies in the later part of the twentieth century reveal that people who pray recover faster from serious illnesses and are less likely to suffer from depression or mental illness. We are human beings—a delicate composition of body and soul, carefully linked by the will and the intellect. Maximum health and well-being of the human person demands that we attend to each of the elements of our being. To ignore the spiritual component of our being necessarily reduces our health, effectiveness, well-being, and efficiency.

Carl Jung, one of this century's most distinguished psychiatrists, in his book Modern Man in Search of A Soul, wrote, *"During the past thirty years, people from all civilized countries of the earth have consulted me. I have treated many hundreds of patients. Among all my patients in the second half of life—that is to say, over thirty-five—there has not been one whose problem in the last resort was not that of finding a religious outlook on life. It is safe to say that every one of them fell ill because he had lost that which the living religions of every age have given to their followers, and none of them has been really healed who did not regain his religious outlook."*

Is it merely a coincidence that, in this age marked by its rejection of religion and spirituality, the incidence of depression and mental illness has escalated so dramatically?

Unfortunately, we live in an age when matters of the spirit are neglected, and in some ways, looked down upon. Faith is a liberating force. Religion is a liberating force. Spirituality is a liberating force. It is natural for human beings to pray: we are naturally spiritual beings. We live in a material world, but we are not solely material.

—⁓—

One hour is a long time. Start with fifteen minutes and gradually work your way up to an hour as you find yourself yearning for more and more of this silence and solitude. It may be hard to believe, but you will. You will yearn and long for this time of prayer. You will look forward to your sacred hour each day. You will find refreshment and peace in this time. You will come to guard and treasure it.

Let this sacred time be a disciplined effort. Start with fifteen minutes, move on to half an hour, and so on. If you are dedicating half an hour to this exercise, don't quit after twenty minutes. As your spirit is settling, it is easy to give in to the restlessness and quit, particularly on busy days. Remember, every disciplined effort has its own multiple reward.

—⁓—

If you read every book ever written on baseball, would that make you the greatest baseball player ever? You only learn to ride a bicycle by riding a bicycle, to play football by playing football, to cook by cooking. You only become a great baseball player by playing baseball. Prayer is a lot like love. We are born with a natural ability and capacity to love. This ability to love develops when we exercise it. We learn to love by loving. The only way to learn to pray is to pray. Books, teachers, guides, mentors, role models, and coaches all help to perfect our abilities, but there is no substitute for the actual practice—whether it is baseball, cooking, football, love, or prayer.

As I write these words about prayer, the words of Henry David Thoureau echo in my mind. *"I went to the woods because I wanted to live deliberately... I wanted to live deep and suck out all of the marrow of life! To put to rout all that was not life. And not, when I came to die, discover that I had not lived..."*

I go to the woods of prayer each day because I want to live life deliberately. I pray because I want to live life deeply and suck out all the marrow of life! I go to prayer to put to rout all that is not life, to separate those things that are important from those that are of little or no consequence. I go to the woods of prayer, because I do not want to come to die and discover that I have not lived.

Go to the woods of prayer. Go to the classroom of silence. From these places you will emerge capable of living life to the fullest—attuned and empowered to live life deliberately.

———

In December of 1993 I traveled to Ireland for the first time. For almost a month I gave talks across the country to small groups and large groups. It was my first international speaking trip and my first Christmas away from home. I was twenty years old and had never seen a white Christmas. I spent that Christmas in Ireland with a man who has since become one of my dearest friends. We sat by the fire and told stories, and the stories ignited a fire within us. We both share a passion for stories and storytelling. This is one of the stories he told me that Christmas.

———

There was once a troubadour. We are told he was a startlingly handsome man, with beautiful olive skin and raven black hair, with eyes as green as river reeds, with long thick lashes. He was very handsome in every way, full of the tone and sinew of youth. His family, rich and respected, dressed him in the finest threads and velvets, and his popularity among the ladies was unmatched. He had everything, didn't have to work for a living, and had a host of comrades who loved and adored him.

He went as a brave soldier to war with the blessings of the whole town. When in battle, he was laughing with his friends as he engaged the enemy, looking on it as a sort of game. In fact, he was so self-confident in the middle of danger that he was knocked from his horse, and while unconscious was dragged by his foot which was caught in the stirrup. When he came to, it was night. He was near a small pool of water in a clearing, the horse was grazing, his foot still caught. He was on his back and looking up into the sky. It was one of those very black nights, with no moon, but a few very bright stars. Everywhere there was silence. He gazed up at one of the stars and his whole life and its meaning passed before him for assessment.

He went unconscious again and the fever raged in his body for weeks. Eventually he returned to his family, and they kept vigil by his bedside as they felt each hour might be his last. Many visitors came to see him—priests, bishops, the town mayor, even a cardinal.

At last, one morning, those river reed green eyes opened up to the sound of a bird on the window singing. All he wanted to do was hold the bird closer and listen to its song. Weak as he was, he got out of bed and tried to catch the bird, but it fled from him, off the window sill and onto the roof opposite his room. At that moment he remembered the midnight sky, and the last thing he remembered was looking up at that bright star while his life flashed before him.

This young man was so loved and revered by his family and all the townspeople that shortly afterwards they gave him a great party to celebrate his return to health. From far and wide, all the family's friends traveled to join the celebration, but he was changed. All the things he used to do with his friends he found he could no longer enjoy, and all the dazzling clothes his parents put on him he had no interest in. All he could think about was that night sky and the bright star. And when they would catch him in this reverie and ask him what he was so preoccupied with, and he would tell them, they'd shove another brew in front of him and say, "You'll get over it."

Every day this man could not wait to get out of the city into the countryside, into the fields of flowers. One day he lay on the ground and put his fingers and toes into the very moist earth of the meadow, and he stayed there with his face in the ground the whole afternoon. Another day he found a stone that was marbled in glittering dust, and he stared at it all day. This was a very different person from the happy-go-lucky warrior that set out for battle a short while before.

He spent all his days in the countryside and his parents knew they were losing him; that wonderful son on whom they depended to carry on the family, to take over the family businesses, and perhaps one day to become governor of the province. He smiles at them and he loves them, but little by little they were losing him.

Then one day he realized how much he loved God. The God who did not say anything in the dark midnight sky, but was there, the God who was in the bird that sang a song to his awakening, and in the moist and good earth that allowed him just to lie there, and in the poppies that dazzled his eyes with blazing scarlet colors and the humming of bees and the iridescence of butterfly wings. He realized that this God he loved was the unseen gift all around him. His parents thought he had gone off the deep end and threw endless parties to try to get him to snap out of it. They even sent him to talk to the priests, who only shook their heads.

Finally, one day at a great party, when he was dressed in the most dazzling clothes his parents could procure for him, he stripped down naked in front of all the assembly, minister, priests, family, women, friends, goats and sheep, the sky, the earth, the village. Not that he was an exhibitionist; no, it was a sign that he didn't belong to this life any more, and he ran from the city with a song in his heart to find some cloth of the field to cover his body. There was a song in his heart and a gentle spirit which was born of the fever. Later he would find an old place and begin to build it up with stones, through freezing winter rains. His worship to the glory of God was the kingdom of the earth.

The greatest contribution that the midnight sky made to him was not the image for which he had lived so long, but the true beauty within man and woman. The fever burned away the image so that he could see what he had never seen before. He turned the page and changed. His parents could no longer see in him the camaraderie they lacked in themselves. The women could no longer see in him the need for a lover that they lacked in their own lives. He changed and they couldn't see in him anymore what they were themselves. They would have to grow to find in him what was in themselves all along.

What was now looking out from those green eyes was not the image, but the magnificent light he had become. He would walk in the fields and the birds and the animals would go to him. Once a great mountain lion came and lay at his feet. Why did he call these things brothers and sisters? Because they were. A wild animal will not lie down beside a person devoted to the image, because the image is the stagnation of regressive energy, copulation, pain, fear, doubt, and power. But a lion will lie down peacefully at the feet of a great light and find a oneness with it, because the light that it sees and senses is the life force of its very being.

This man lived the rest of his life being a glory of God, a glory to the God who had emerged in him. He sang of the glory of life and tried to educate people, not in doctrine, but in the simplicity of knowledge. He lived no hypocrisies but was devoted only to God. He became hated and despised, because he tried to shine in the darkness while other people guarded the light switch.

This is a true story. The dashing young man was Francis of Assisi.

—◦∿◦—

There is no greater force to live by than faith. Prayer gives us vision, courage, strength, and endurance. Prayer dissolves our prejudices, banishes our narrow mindedness,

and melts away our judgmental tendencies by expanding our hearts, minds, and spirits.

We pray to God on our knees—but we also pray in
peace, joy, love, and laughter.

Life is prayer.

Perhaps now would be a good time to take a couple
of minutes to pray. This is the rest of the prayer Francis
wrote in the twelfth century. Born in Assisi in Italy,
he was the founder of the Franciscan Order of Friars.
He had a profound love of nature, and approached all
living beings, creatures, and entities as brothers and
sisters. His prayer is as profound and powerful today as
it has ever been.

> Lord, make me an instrument of your *peace*.
> where there is hatred, let me sow *love*.
> where there is injury, let me sow *pardon*;
> where there is doubt, let me sow *faith*;
> where there is despair, let me sow *hope*;
> where there is darkness, let me sow *light*; and
> where there is sadness, let me sow *joy*.
>
> Divine Master, grant that I may not so much seek
> to be consoled as to console;
> to be understood as to understand;
> to be loved as to love;
> for it is in giving that we receive,
> it is in pardoning that we are pardoned,
> and it is in dying that we are born to eternal life.

THE SEVENTH DAY

Wouldn't it be nice to have one day a week just to rest,
reflect, and be renewed? Would you be happier, health-

ier, maybe even a better person? What is stopping you? I believe that honoring *The Seventh Day* makes sense even for an atheist.

The Rhythm of Life is founded by ancient tradition, eternal mysteries, modern knowledge, and common sense.

The Seventh Day has its roots in the Judeo-Christian scriptures and tradition. As discussed in Chapter Four, in the book of Genesis we read, "On the seventh day God rested from all the work that he had done." Why did God rest on the seventh day? Was God tired? Of course not. God did not need to rest, but he foresaw our "need" for rest. In foreseeing our need for rest God established *The Seventh Day* as a holy day to be set aside for rest and renewal.

God did not create the Sabbath for His sake. God created the Sabbath for our sake. The Sabbath doesn't help God, it helps us.

By instituting *The Seventh Day* as a day of rest and renewal, by setting this time aside, God provided another instrument to restore and maintain rhythm in our lives—*The Rhythm of Life* that gives birth to peace, harmony, effective living, and optimum health and well-being.

The Third Instrument

The First and Second Instruments help us to find *The Rhythm of Life* day by day. The Third Instrument—*The Seventh Day*—helps us to anchor our weeks in *The Rhythm of Life*. Here, we will discuss *The Seventh Day* as a time of rest and renewal, and as an instrument in creating and maintaining a rhythm in our lives which

enables us to achieve and maintain our maximum capacity in every area of our lives.

—〰〰—

The Seventh Day is an ancient tradition founded and
based on our most human needs. It is a Jewish tradition
and a Christian tradition. Other religious traditions also
honor one day of the week as a day of worship and rest.
In this age which has not been kind to tradition, I believe there is a great need to embrace this wonderful,
life-giving tradition of *The Seventh Day*.

The tradition of the Sabbath emerged from our legitimate need as human beings for rest. *The Seventh Day*
tradition upholds, protects, and ensures our legitimate
need for rest and relaxation, for a change of pace, for
time with family and friends, for time to turn toward
the transcendental, and for time to renew our connection with God. It is a tradition as relevant today as it
was five thousand years ago.

—〰〰—

The modern conception of life only respects action. To
be spending your time in a worthwhile manner you
must be doing or achieving something. The crudest
and most basic measure of this attitude is money-mak-
ing. This mind-set affects even the way we spend our
recreation time. People are so caught up in this obses-
sion with action and activity, that they feel they must
be doing something constantly. It is for this reason that
prayer is neglected by the masses during this time.
Prayer is an inner activity. When you pray you take on
the appearance of doing nothing. And because the
fruits, benefits, and rewards of prayer are internal, you

appear to be achieving nothing. Nothing could be further from the truth.

Not every person with their eyes closed is asleep, and not every person with their eyes open can see.

Our political, social, and cultural movements do not uphold the journey from *Point A* to *Point B*. The philosophical foundation of the lifestyles celebrated by the modern media screams out, "Life is about what you have and what you do." Pleasure, possessions, and power are the three pillars of this philosophy. The emphasis is on having and doing, rather than on becoming. The truth is, what you become is infinitely more important than what you do, or what you have.

The Third Instrument invites us to set aside one day each week to relax and refocus, to remind ourselves of the priorities of our lives. One day a week to turn our backs to the wind, to dust the dirt from our feet and our souls, to drift and dream, and to open ourselves to peace, tranquility, leisure, and simple appreciation of life.

Be creative. There are thousands of ways to spend *The Seventh Day*. Broaden your horizons.

Paint a picture.

Read poetry.

Write a poem.

Take an afternoon nap.

Spend time with your family.

Make some memories.

Go to church.

Read one of those books you have been meaning to read for years.

Speak your love.

Get a little exercise.

Spend time with your friends.

Eat a nice big bowl of chocolate ice cream.
Fall in love again with life.
Visit someone who is lonely.
Write in your journal.
Find the time.
Just sit and listen to music.
If you can play, play.
Music is therapeutic, it refreshes the spirit.
Give a massage.
Get a massage.
Go fishing.
Plant a garden.
Eat some chocolate.
Cloud watch.
Watch the children at play in the local playground.
Lay on a beach and soak up the sun.
Seek out a forgotten friend.
Talk by the fire.
Run.
Speak your love again.
Watch a movie together.
Sleep under the stars.
Laugh a little.
Laugh a little more.
Go to a play.
Apologize for always being so busy.
Visit a museum or an art gallery.
Listen.
Go back and read the novels you studied in your last year of high school.
Dance slowly, arm in arm.
Swim.
Get to bed early.

Visit with solitude.

Befriend silence.

Ponder and absorb the thoughts of poets, philosophers, sages, seers, and saints.

Follow the advice of Dostoevsky, the famed Russian novelist, who wrote, *"The soul is healed by being with children."*

Go for a picnic.

Keep a promise.

Learn to play a musical instrument.

Walk in the park.

Watch a sunset.

Listen to the rain.

Write a love letter.

Bake some cookies...

———

It is these types of activities that renew us, refresh us, bring rhythm to our lives, lead us toward maximum health, liberate our hearts and minds, and remind us of who we are and what is really important.

Fill *The Seventh Day* with enriching experiences that bring new meaning and depth to your life. Step back and get a good look at life, and then, immerse yourself more fully in it.

A good starting point would be to try to do at least one activity in each of the four areas of legitimate need—physical, emotional, intellectual, and spiritual—on *The Seventh Day*.

———

Everything happens according to the seasons. Nature is based on certain cycles. These cycles are the untapped power of our lives. If a farmer plants the seed in the winter will he have a crop in the spring? No, he will have wasted his time, effort, energy, and seed. It is knowledge of the cycles, seasons, and rhythms of nature that makes a farmer successful.

Today, it is common knowledge and practice that a rested field yields a plentiful crop. I wonder, the first time a farmer decided to let a field rest for a year, did his neighbors and friends say, "Oh, that's a clever idea"? Absolutely not. They laughed at him, made fun of him, talked about him behind his back, and thought he was crazy. The next year when he brought in his crop from that field, he had the last laugh. The following year when there were three or four fields resting, he smiled to himself with a gentle sense of quiet satisfaction. Ten years later when every farmer in the district was using the resting field method, he had become a legend.

The cycles of nature hold the untapped power of our lives too. As you begin to discover those cycles and live by them your friends will think you are crazy for leaving the party early, or passing up "an irresistible opportunity" at work, or for changing the way you spend your Sunday. But over the weeks, months, and years ahead, as you bring the harvest of your life to be weighed, they will soon see that your way is better. They will turn to it. They too will begin to seek *The Rhythm of Life*.

—⁓—

The question becomes: Are you prepared to give your health and happiness priority over your bank balance and your toy collection? *The Rhythm of Life* should be a priority in our lives. *The Seventh Day* as a day of rest is a very powerful tool in creating and maintaining *The Rhythm of Life*. Acknowledge the wisdom behind the Sabbath tradition. Use this day. Accept this gift. Allow this day of rest to regulate your week, to provide a macro-rhythm for your life.

Do you ever feel like you just need a day off? A day to relax, to be with family and friends, to do nothing at all, a day to take it easy? Embrace *The Seventh Day*.

Allow yourself to be renewed and refreshed. For thousands of years wise men and women of every culture have been tapping the power of the Sabbath, in one form or another, to maintain rhythm in their lives. From this rest and reflection of *The Seventh Day* we emerge with a keen sense of what our priorities are, and return to our work and to the world, rooted once again in our life principles.

——~~~——

There once lived a man whose name was Jude. He was an apostle of Jesus Christ and was renowned throughout the region as a wise and deeply spiritual man. People traveled great distances, venturing across foreign lands to seek his advice and healing.

One day Jude was relaxing outside his hut when a hunter came by. The hunter was surprised to see Jude relaxing, and rebuffed him for loafing. It was not the hunter's idea of what a holy man should be doing.

Jude recognized these thoughts running through the hunter's mind and also noticed that the man carried a bow for hunting. "What is your occupation sir?" Jude asked. "I am a hunter," he replied. "Very good," Jude said, "Bend your bow and shoot an arrow." The man did so. "Bend it again and shoot another arrow," said Jude. The hunter did so, again and again. Finally he complained, "Father, if I keep my bow always stretched it will break."

"Very good my child," Jude replied, "So it is with me and all people, if we push ourselves beyond measure, we will break. It is good and right from time to time to relax and recreate ourselves."

—◦◦◦—

If you don't break from the tensions of daily living, they will break you.

—◦◦◦—

What is music made of? Yes, of course rhythm. What else? Yes, notes. When you write music, do you write only notes? No. In music the rests are as important as the notes. Great musicians know the power of rest. If you listen to a great public speaker, you will discover that the way that person pauses is as powerful as the words he speaks. It is true also in life. The rests are as important as the activity. The silence is as important as the noise. The rest makes the activity more powerful and efficient. The silence makes the noise more meaningful.

Walt Whitman once wrote, *"I loaf and invite my soul."* Loafing opens the heart and mind to allow peace and tranquility to flow in. We all need a time to relax and listen to the voice within which reveals the truth that makes us free.

Leisure increases the richness of life. The wise make time to loaf. In this modern age obsessed with noise and movement we seem incapable of relaxing. Take it easy.

Let us conclude our discussion with a reflection from Leonardo da Vinci. Born in Italy 1452, da Vinci was a

painter, sculptor, architect, musician, engineer, mathematician, and scientist. Leonardo da Vinci was unquestionably one of the greatest intellects in human history.

Every now and then go away,
   have a little relaxation,
   for when you come back to your work
   your judgement will be surer;
   since to remain constantly at work
   will cause you to lose power of judgement ...

Go some distance away
   because the work appears smaller and
   more of it can be taken in at a glance,
   and a lack of harmony
   or proportion
   is more readily seen.

THE ART OF SLOWING DOWN

There is an art to slowing down. In our busy world it is
not easy to master this art, but necessary. Our lives have
a habit of gathering a momentum of their own, plung-
ing forward, with or without our consent. Learn to slow
down and access life. Take your foot off the accelerator
and look about, and within.

Slow down. Breathe deeply. Reflect deeply. Pray
deeply. Live deeply. Otherwise, you will spend your
life feeling like a bulldozer chasing butterflies, or a
sparrow in a hurricane.

CHAPTER 6

THE WAY

I don't know where it came from, or why I developed it, but for as long as I can remember it has been a part of me. I have always been fascinated with famous and successful people.

When I was a child, I often dreamed of being a sports star. So I looked to my sporting heroes—soccer champion, Pele; golfing great, Greg Norman; and cricket legend, Don Bradman; and I thought to myself, "I hope that happens to me one day."

As I grew older, my fascination with famous people expanded to include men and women from all walks of life—movie stars, entrepreneurs, politicians, religious leaders, musicians and artists. I began to read about them and watch movies and documentaries about their lives and work. I studied their lives with an insatiable curiosity.

As I look back now I realize I was searching for clues. I wanted to know the secrets of their success. What makes a champion a champion? Over time I began to see how their success was achieved. Whether it was to make one hundred million dollars, to become a world-class football player, to raise a wonderful family, to become a great political leader, to be an inspirational artist or author, or to live a life of heroic holiness—I discovered that for the most part all of these people possessed a basic set of qualities. Their success wasn't just good luck. I began to see a pattern emerge. Regardless of their field, each of them applied a set of principles to their individual and unique situations, which produced phenomenal results.

There is a pattern. It is what leaders, legends, heroes, great achievers, champions, and saints do to excel in their given field. This is *The Way*, from start to finish. Let me tell you about the way I believe they achieve it.

———

The first thing they do is work out where they are— *Point A*—and who they are—*Self Knowledge*. They take a good long hard look at themselves. They establish their needs, talents, and desires. They define and list their strengths and weaknesses. They define who they are and where they are. They write it down.

The very next thing they do, is work out where they want to go—*Point B*. They call that their dream, their goal, or their ambition. They define it precisely and they write it down. They *Dream*.

Now that they know where they are and who they are—*Point A*—and where they want to go—*Point B*—they establish which path will take them there the quickest. They Have a Vision. Then they begin to walk that path.

As they walk that path they allow all of their actions to be guided by a *Life Principle* which summarizes in one sentence their purpose and ambition.

Every morning when they wake up the first thing they do is remind themselves of their goal. Every night before they go to bed, the last thing they do is remind themselves of their goal. They remind themselves of that goal in every waking moment, of every hour, of every single day. They never let that goal out of their sight. They *Harness the Power of Common Thought.*

They do not let anything get between them and their goal. They are *Dedicated* to their path and plan. They walk the path with unrelenting energy. They begin to use all of their time, effort, and energy in the pursuit of their goal.

If something does come between them and their goal, they consider it an obstacle, and they find a way to go over it, under it, around it, or through it. Guardians of the threshold try to hold them back, delay them, discourage them, and persuade them to walk other paths. But they resist distraction. They *Believe* in their path and plan.

They realize they cannot do it alone. They take time to love and be loved. They *Cherish People*—realizing that nothing worthwhile can be achieved without the love and help of others.

They are infectious. Everything they do and say communicates the passion and vision of their dream.

They *Master Communication*. Who they are, what they do, and how they do it conveys a powerful message.

They experience difficulties and heartache, but they push on, always keeping sight of their goal. They meet and become intimate with real pain and deep suffering, but they resist the temptation to become bitter and jaded. They fall, but they get back up. They fall again, but they get back up again. They fall over and over, but every time they do they get back up. They persevere, and they persevere, and they persevere. They *Never Give Up*.

In time they reach their goal, they grasp their dream, they achieve their ambition. It is not luck. It is not freak chance. Success, achievement, excellence, and greatness are not accidents. They are not just gifts from God for a favored few. They are the fruit of discipline. They are the result of a well implemented formula. There is a formula.

—∿∿—

When we witness success and achievement in other people's lives, the temptation is to belittle it. We may say to ourselves, "Well, to be a major league baseball player is not the most noble goal," or "To be rich and famous, that's not the most noble goal." The question becomes: Do we even have a goal? Do we even have a *Point B* in our lives? Or, are we just wandering around in circles at *Point A*, enslaving ourselves to all types of self-destructive behavior and thinking to ourselves, "I hope that happens to me one day," or "I would give my whole life to be able to do that?"

—∿∿—

Take for example Itzhak Perlman, whom we discussed briefly in Chapter Two. Do you think he ever said to himself, "What is the least I can do and still become the finest violinist in the world?"

To hear Itzhak Perlman play the violin is not just a concert. It is an experience. It is an eclipse—a symphony of sensory and spiritual delight. Itzhak Perlman does something much more than play the violin brilliantly. How do you suppose he came to be so gifted?

Every morning Itzhak Perlman wakes up at five-fifteen. He showers, has a light breakfast, and begins his morning practice session, which lasts for four and a half hours. He has lunch, reads for a while, exercises, then begins his afternoon practice session which lasts for four and a half hours. In the evening, he has dinner and relaxes with his family. This is Itzhak Perlman's schedule every single day of the year, except for on concert days.

On the day of a concert he wakes up at five-fifteen, showers, has breakfast, and begins his morning practice session, which lasts for four and a half hours. He has lunch, reads for a while, exercises, and takes a nap for ninety minutes. When he wakes, he gets dressed and goes to the concert venue. There they perform a sound check and have a brief rehearsal. Forty-five minutes before the concert, Mr. Perlman is found alone in his dressing room. Two security guards are placed outside the locked door with the explicit instructions to let no one in under any circumstances.

What do you think he does?

He prays. Itzhak Perlman prays. How do you think Itzhak chooses to pray at this time? Do you think he says, "God, will you please let me play the violin brilliantly tonight?" This could be, but it is not the type of petition that leaves Itzhak wondering if God will answer his prayer. When Itzhak Perlman says to God, "Will you please let me play the violin brilliantly tonight?" he does not doubt for one single moment that God will answer his prayer.

Why? Because Itzhak Perlman plays the violin brilliantly for nine hours a day, every single day, day in and day out, in an empty room, for nobody but his God. Itzhak Perlman upholds his part of the deal. Passion. Dedication. Belief. So when Itzhak Perlman says, "God, will you please let me play the violin brilliantly tonight?" he knows with absolute certitude that God will answer his prayer.

Is that the end of Perlman's prayer? Absolutely not. So how does he spend the other forty-four minutes of prayer? Itzhak Perlman then visualizes what he wants to take place at the concert that night—how he wants to harness his brilliant performance. Do you think he merely thinks to himself, "I'll go out to the middle of the stage, play the violin, the people will all stand up and clap, and then we will all go home."? Absolutely not. He visualizes exactly what he wants to achieve; he visualizes much more.

Because Itzhak Perlman doesn't just play the violin brilliantly. He reaches into the very depths of people. He grasps a hold of their souls and lifts them up as high as he can. Itzhak Perlman makes people cry and they don't know why they are crying. He makes people feel and hear things they have never felt or heard before— things that cannot be put into words, but must be witnessed and experienced to be understood and believed. He shares his excitement and passion for life through his music, filling his audience with an inexpressible joy. He energizes people. He inspires people. He moves people. He motivates people. He touches people. He changes people. In his own way, he makes a difference in people's lives. And having raised their souls up, he sends them home, knowing that he has instilled in them an excitement and passion for life that is almost uncontainable.

Moments of genius. The inexpressible expressed.

That is what he visualizes in his prayer. You would be mistaken to think that Itzhak Perlman aspires to just play the violin.

Later that night, Itzhak Perlman lies in bed at his hotel, and just before he goes to sleep a gentle smile comes across his face. He is filled with the quiet satisfaction of knowing that all around that city there are men and women tossing and turning in their beds, because they cannot get to sleep. They cannot sleep because their lives have been changed.

Itzhak Perlman has found a way to touch other people's lives, to raise others up, to share his passion for life. He knows that there is no greater satisfaction and fulfillment than to make a difference in another person's life—and that is what it is all about.

Sit in a dark room, turn the volume up, and listen to the theme from the movie *Schindler's List*. It is the first song on the soundtrack, and you will know that it is not by chance that Itzhak Perlman has achieved excellence, success, and greatness.

SUCCESS

If you ask most people what they want from life, as I have taken to doing in recent years, you will discover that they want to achieve success. Some people want to be successful in the workplace and others on the sporting field. Some want to be successful parents and others want to be successful at living their beliefs or the practice of their spirituality. But, if you ask all these people to define success, you will end up with as many different answers as there are people.

The *Oxford Dictionary* defines success as: the accomplishment of an aim; favorable outcome; or, the attainment of wealth, fame, or position.

If this is what success is, please, please tell me there is more to life than success. Or, tell me that success is something else, something more.

"There is only one success—to be able to spend your life in your own way," was Christopher Morley's observation. Mark Twain counseled, *"The secret of success is to make your vocation your vacation."* Ralph Waldo Emerson's definition of success is perhaps the most famed. He wrote, *"To laugh often and much; to win the respect of intelligent people and the affection of children; to earn the appreciation of honest critics and endure the betrayal of false friends; to appreciate beauty, to find the best in others; to leave the world a bit better, whether by a healthy child, a garden patch, or a redeemed social condition; to know even one life has breathed easier because you have lived. This is to have succeeded."*

Ultimately, I suppose each of us must define success for him or herself.

The Rhythm of Life is a foundation for success. Once we lay this foundation in our lives everything we turn our hands to will be successful. But more importantly, we will find a happiness that is rare, true, and lasting.

As a child I discovered that the key to success in any field is not a secret. There are no secrets to success.

Gimmicks and quick fixes do not lead a person to success. Nor do fast-talking empty philosophies. Success in any field—business, sport, politics, music, art, or spirituality, depends upon a deep and profound understanding of who you are, and what your needs, talents, and desires are.

The key to success is character. The key to *your* success is *your* character. And while the foundation of character is self-discipline, the essence of character is personality. Your own unique personality holds the secrets to your success.

—◢◣◤◥—

I believe the greatest success is to be constantly growing, changing, developing, evolving into the better person I know I can be. In any activity that assists you in this "becoming" you will find success. Why? In the long run you won't be successful at something you don't enjoy doing. Enjoyment is an indispensable ingredient for success. We are successful at the things we enjoy, the endeavors we love, the labors we are excited and passionate about. It is easy to be passionate about the things that challenge us to become the better person we know we can be.

Before too long we become bored, dissatisfied, and discontent with any activity that cannot be employed as a tool in the process of growth and development.

—◢◣◤◥—

Success is the intimate and harmonious relationship between need, desire, and talent. When these three are understood and pursued in balance the result is extraordinary.

Mozart had a great talent, but he also had a burning desire to make music, and a great need, as do we all, to touch other people's lives. The delicate blend of these three—need, desire, and talent—produced a result that leaves us awestruck, even today more than two hundred years after his death.

Do you remember in school when you would write an essay? You would begin by writing a rough draft and then you would write a more polished version of your piece. Perhaps you would even write a third, fourth, and fifth draft before writing a final draft to hand in to your teacher.

Mozart never made copies of his music. Mozart never wrote a rough draft. No copies. No drafts. No practices. No corrections. Just a final manuscript. Just the brilliance you hear in his music on paper the first time he wrote it down. That, my friends, is extraordinary. It is greatness. It is a phenomenal blend of need, desire, and talent. It is an unfathomable mixture of genius, legend, heroism, passion, and prophecy. It is nothing less than the Divine shining through a human being.

He lived only 36 years. In that brief lifetime Mozart composed six first-rate operas, 21 piano concertos, 24 string quartets, 17 Masses, assorted chamber music and other solo concertos. And of course, 41 symphonies.

Chance? Luck? I don't think so. Passion. Discipline. Perseverance. Commitment.

—⁓—

Creating the rhythm is about setting the stage for your needs, desires, and talents to emerge, to be understood, and to be fulfilled. *The Rhythm of Life* allows us to know, understand, and pursue each of these—need, desire, and talent. The result is success, yes—but an elevated success of which most people of the world do not know—the kind of success which brings with it fulfillment, satisfaction, happiness, health, a deep and abiding peace, and the unalterable reward of becoming 'the better person you know you can be.'

We desire success, fulfillment, happiness and to become better people, but we torment ourselves. We do this by failing to find the appropriate relationship between need, desire, and talent. We rush off in pursuit of "success!" Many men and women find some type of "success"—they make extraordinary amounts of money, or rise to unimaginable levels of fame, but they do not find happiness or fulfillment in that success. Why not?

These people don't understand their needs, they have little understanding of their talents, nor do they seek out their truest and deepest desires. The result is discord, unhappiness, and dissatisfaction. The great juxtaposition of their so-called "success" and their personal dissatisfaction is confusing, even horrifying.

Success is to become who you really are.

A poet must write poetry, an artist must paint, a musician must make music, a lover must love, an athlete must run. When a poet writes poetry, she subconsciously but delicately creates the link between her need, her desire, and her talent. The result, or byproduct, of this great mixture of need, desire, and talent is peace, joy, and a deep sense of satisfaction and fulfillment. For the poet not to write poetry would be insanity. For the poet not to write poetry would quite literally produce insanity.

We become mad by attempting to be other than who we truly are.

We cannot be happy trying to be someone else, however good or great that person may be. We will never find happiness and fulfillment following someone else's dream, however great or noble their dream may be.

True success lies in seeking to discover who you truly are individually and uniquely; finding your own special gift, talent, or ability; and developing that gift for the benefit of all. Such success enriches the individual in every way. This type of success enriches society.

Success is not just an achievement, it is a contribution.

—⁓—

The key to your health and happiness is in finding *The Rhythm of Life* and building your life and success around that rhythm. Whatever you choose to do with the rest of your life, these *Ten Character Principles* will be the key to your success.

In my fascination for famous and successful people, as a child I began to ask: Why do some people succeed and others fail? This questioning led me to look at people who were not successful. Was it lack of desire that separated success from failure? No, it was not. I discovered, in fact, that some people who were not successful desired success more than those who were. I came to see that people don't fail because they want to fail—they fail because they don't know how to succeed. Desire is not enough. Talent is not enough. You must know *The Way*. You need the formula.

This is *The Way*. Here is the formula. Create a lifestyle with *The Rhythm of Life*, and within that context develop the following *Ten Character Principles*.

THE KNOWLEDGE PRINCIPLE

Ralph Waldo Emerson once wrote, *"What lies behind us and what lies before us are small matters compared with what lies within us."* Shakespeare counseled, *"To thine own self be true."* But in order to live Shakespeare's maxim, we must heed the advice of Socrates, *"Know Yourself."*

Lasting success, fulfillment, and happiness depend on self-knowledge. There is no greater practical wisdom than knowledge of self. The Knowledge Principle is simply—*Know Yourself.*

In Chapter Three we asked ourselves these questions: What are my dreams? What are my legitimate needs? What are my desires? What are my talents? What is the relationship between my needs, desires, and talents? Who am I? Am I evolving into a better person each day? What are my addictions? Which path should I take? What star am I following?

All of these questions were designed to challenge us to seek to know ourselves a little more. From this knowledge of ourselves, we are able to create and maintain a lifestyle that intimately links our dreams, hopes, needs, desires, and talents together—while at the same time leading us to change, grow, develop, and become the better person we know we can be.

Wise people know themselves and live from that knowledge. If I know that to be healthy and happy I need seven hours of sleep each night, and I sleep for only five, I am a fool. I am worse than the ignorant person who cannot make the connection between his lack of sleep and his poor health and unhappiness. I possess the knowledge, but do not use it.

There is a Japanese proverb which speaks of the three most valuable possessions in this life. The third is the sword, because it empowers you to defend yourself and those you love from intruders and tyrants. The second is the gem, because it empowers you to buy and trade for the satisfaction of your temporal needs. The Japanese believe the most valuable possession is the mirror, because it empowers you to know yourself.

Great men and women know themselves. They know their strengths, their weaknesses, their faults and failings, their flaws and defects, their talents and abilities, their needs and desires, their hopes and dreams, their potential and purpose. From these pieces of knowledge they weave a life of beauty and splendor. *Know Yourself* is a character principle of legends, heroes, champions, leaders, and saints.

Fear holds us back. We refuse to look in the mirror, not always physically, but emotionally, intellectually, and spiritually. I have heard it said that an alcoholic cannot look himself in the eyes in the mirror. We are scared of what we will find. So we think and talk only of our good qualities and achievements, but in doing so we shun some of life's most rewarding and fulfilling lessons. If only we would take a good look at each of the major areas of our being each day, we would discover our dreams, hopes, needs, desires, talents, and potential. If only we knew what we needed, we would be very wise indeed. But, so often, we refuse to look at anything but our strengths and desires. Weakness and need are much more valuable companions and teachers.

Each day during your *Sacred Hour* take the time to make a daily personal assessment. Ask yourself the difficult questions. Try to discover what makes you feel good about yourself and what makes you happy—not momentary pleasures, but the true pleasures of life which taste better and better as each day passes.

The things of earth compete for our allegiance. To be true to yourself you must form an allegiance with the things of this earth only in as much as they lead you towards your completion, fulfillment, and perfection—*Point B*—to become the better person you know you can be.

To know one's self is a constant and continual process. Observe yourself. Be aware. Watch yourself in the moments of the day. Listen to yourself. Notice how you act or react in certain situations.

The fullness of life comes from knowing yourself—needs, desires, talents, strengths, weaknesses, limitations and potential—and living from the wisdom of this knowledge.

—∾∾—

Perhaps you are familiar with Leonardo da Vinci's famous painting of the Last Supper. da Vinci was living in Milan at the time he painted it, and when he committed himself to that particular composition, Leonardo decided he wanted to approach it in a unique way. He wanted to find thirteen men to pose, one for each of the disciples and one as Jesus. He wanted each of his models to look exactly as he envisioned Jesus and each of the disciples to have looked. And so his search for these men began.

One day while he was sitting in church the voices of the choir were so angelic that he turned around and looked up into the choir loft. As he did his gaze fell upon one young man in the choir. He perfectly matched how da Vinci had visualized Jesus to look. After church Leonardo approached the young man, explained his project, and inquired as to whether he would be interested in posing for the painting. The young man agreed, and the following week he spent four days posing for da Vinci in his studio in Milan.

Da Vinci's search continued and he quickly found someone to pose as Peter, Simon, and Matthew. Within eleven months he had found and painted all the persons in the scene except for Judas.

Da Vinci could not find his Judas. He looked everywhere. He would walk through the streets of Milan, some days for endless hours, searching the nameless faces in the crowds for a man who embodied how he envisioned Judas to have looked. Eleven years passed in his search for Judas when he finally realized he had been looking for his Judas in the wrong places.

Leonardo thought to himself, if I am to find a man who has the qualities and appearance of Judas, I must look where such men are gathered. With that in mind da Vinci went to the prisons in and around Milan, searching for a man with pain and anger in his eyes, with harsh impatience on his face, with the scars of pride and bitterness on his cheeks, and the marks of brokeness in his features—a man who looked to him like Judas.

After many days and many prisons he came across that man. He explained to the man what he was doing and asked him if he would be willing to pose for the painting. The prisoner agreed and Leonardo made arrangements for him to be brought to his studio in Milan under guard.

The following week he was brought to the studio and da Vinci began the final stage of his work. As he painted, da Vinci noticed that the prisoner was growing more restless and distressed, even by the hour. Da Vinci observed that the man would look at him, and then at the painting, and every time seemed to be filled with a certain remorseful sadness.

By the middle of the second day Leonardo was so disturbed by what he was witnessing in his model that he stopped work and said to him, "Is there something wrong? Do you not like my work?" The prisoner said nothing and da Vinci inquired once more saying, "You seem very upset and if I am causing you pain in any way perhaps we should stop." The man looked at the master painter and then at the painting one more time. As his gaze fell away from the painting, he lowered his head, lifted his hands to his face and began to weep inconsolably.

After several minutes da Vinci was finally able to settle him. "What is it?" he asked. The prisoner looked expectantly into the artist's eyes and said, "Do you not recognize me, Master?" In confusion Leonardo replied, "No, have we met before?" "Oh yes," the prisoner explained, "Eleven years ago I posed for you, for this same painting, as the person of Jesus."

In each of us there is a Judas and a Jesus, a Peter, a John, and a Matthew. Our lives here on earth are an incomplete work unless we can discover the Judas within us, come to know that person in us, and paint the details of that person. It is only with knowledge of our character flaws and defects that we can work to overcome them. Are you prepared to face the Judas in you?

—◊◊—

When God was creating the universe some of the angels were discussing where they each felt God should hide the truth. One angel said, "I think God should hide the truth at the very summit of the highest mountain." The next proclaimed, "I think God should hide the truth at the very depths of the ocean." Another said, "No, I think God should hide the truth on the furthest star."

God overheard the angels and spoke up, saying, "I will hide the truth in none of these places. I will hide the truth at the very depths of every man and every woman's heart. This way, those who search humbly and sincerely will find it very easily, and those that do not, will have to search the whole universe before they do."

—◊◊—

Know thyself; know your strengths and weaknesses; your relation to the universe; your potentialities; your spiritual heritage; your aims and purposes; take stock of thyself.

—Socrates

THE DREAM PRINCIPLE

Life, in a sense, is a long succession of choices and decisions. How do you make your decisions? On what do you base your decisions? Do you have a process that you trust and use faithfully?

In a similar sense, life is made up of hopes and dreams. You dream the dreams and you make the decisions. From an infinite number of possibilities you must decide how to spend your life. The form your life takes depends on the decisions you make.

What is different about the way legends, heroes, champions, leaders, and saints make decisions? What is their decision making process?

They allow themselves to dream. They imagine perfect circumstances. They place no limitations upon their decision making process. They ask: What would be best? What is the will of God? If I could do anything, what would I do?

Most people base their decisions on the limited resources available to them at the present moment. For example, Ralph is a senior in high school and wants to go to college. The first question he asks himself is, "What colleges can I afford?" After gathering that data he then makes a decision based on the options he perceives are available to him.

Legends, heroes, champions, leaders, and saints ask themselves, "Which college would be most suited to my needs? Which college will most help me grow and become the better person I know I can be? Which college will most assist me in the pursuit of my dreams?" And, before they make decisions, they employ The Dream Principle—they *Dream Without Limit*. They remove themselves from space and time. They remove all limitation from the initial stage of their decision process. If they discover that the best college for them is Yale, and that Yale costs $20,000 a year more than they can afford, they don't throw out the best option, they find a way to get the money. If they only have a 3.4 grade point average and to get into Yale they need a 3.7, they don't abandon the best option and their dream. They find a way. They go to another college for a semester and increase their grade point average.

The great people of history remove all limitation from their dreams, and once they establish their dream, they seek it with unrelenting energy.

Do not dream like a bank manager. A bank manager only tells you what you can afford based on your realized potential. The greater part of all of us is our un-realized potential. It is true—physically, emotionally, intellectually, and spiritually. Do not let the guardians of the threshold prevent you from moving on and grasping your dreams. Do not let the emotional, intel-lectual, and spiritual bank managers discourage you from becoming the better person you know you can be.

Try also not to allow your dreams and decisions be formed, affected, or guided by fear, anger, hatred, greed, or lust. It takes courage to dream, because most of us have an awful fear of failure. Our fear of failure confines us to the dim gray twilight of life. We allow phrases like, "What if I fail?" and "I can't do it" to infect our inner dialogue.

The human spirit thrives on victory, growth, change, and development—and all of these involve making the impossible, possible. Eleanor Roosevelt wrote, *"You must do things you cannot do. It strengthens character, builds courage and strength, confidence and belief."*

Columbus, Einstein, Edison, Rakhmaninoff, Henry Ford, the Wright Brothers—the dreamers of the dreams—they made the unknown known, the impossible possible.
Dream Without Limits.

———

On my desk at home where I write I have a photograph of myself when I was seven years old. It is always amusing to watch how different people react to the photo once they discover it is not my little brother or nephew, but rather myself. Some perhaps think me vain and egotistical. Some wonder and others ask, "Why?"

My seventh year was very special. It was the year that set the stage for the rest of my life. It was the year that I learned life's first lesson. It was the year I learned to love life. If you have heard me speak you have perhaps heard me tell this story. If you have read some of my other writings you have perhaps read it in one form or another. I beg your indulgence as I tell it once more.

First grade was the best and the worst two years of my life. I didn't seem to have any friends, and those I thought were my friends seemed to always be making fun of me. One day, one of the cool kids called me "ugly" and that seemed to stick as a nick name. Apart from all this I had one other problem which was seriously troubling me.

In first grade I remember week after week on Friday afternoons coming to the school gate and finding three or four of my brothers standing around waiting for my mother. They were always very happy and excited because once again, the school week was over and the weekend had begun. But week after week on Friday afternoon, I found myself coming to the school gate sad.

I can still recall one Friday afternoon in particular. The school bell rang and everyone rushed out of class and ran towards the gates. I gathered my things together slowly, packed my school bag, tidied my desk, and then dragged my bag slowly towards the school gate where I found four of my brothers. Once again they were very happy and excited because the weekend had come around. That Friday afternoon I was particularly sad.

I remember my mother coming to pick us up. We all walked down the street to where she had parked the car, and as we got close she took our bags from us and put them in the back. One by one we got into the car and as I climbed in I burst into tears. I had been holding the tears back all afternoon, and I couldn't hold them back any longer. My brothers looked at me, wondering what had happened, and when my mother saw me crying, she said, "What's wrong?"

In first grade on Friday afternoons we had our spelling test. Between sobs I explained to my mother that I had failed my spelling test again. I always failed. I couldn't spell. That day my mother took me home and held me in her arms and said, "Everything is going to be alright. We will practice your spelling and you will get better."

Then she said to me, "How many did you get in your spelling test today?" And I said, "Six out of twenty." My mum said, "That's fine. If you get seven next week, on Friday afternoon I will take you straight from school and buy you a big bar of chocolate." The next Friday I got seven, and I got my bar of chocolate. In the following weeks—eight, nine, ten, and more chocolate. Twelve, fourteen, sixteen, and still more chocolate. Eighteen, nineteen, twenty, and even more chocolate. Until finally I had developed a love for chocolate, and I could spell.

I could spell. I had made the impossible, possible. I had climbed my Mount Everest, I had walked on the moon, I had won my Olympic gold medal.

For me, at the age of seven, I believed my chances of learning to spell were less than most people's chances of climbing Mount Everest or walking on the moon. It just seemed impossible. It was too big and I was too small. But on that day when I first scored twenty out of twenty on my spelling test, I realized I had achieved the impossible. I wasn't aware of it at the time, but my life changed forever that day, and as the days and weeks passed I developed a deep belief that I was capable of anything. I had achieved the impossible, and impossible had been deleted from my vocabulary.

I began to dream without limits.

The following year I repeated first grade, made wonderful friends, continued to do well in spelling, and began to really enjoy life. The journey continues. That photo sits on my desk to remind me of first grade, to remind me that I am capable of even the things that seem impossible.

It is through the mastery of small disciplines that we become capable of greater things, and indeed, anything.

THE VISION PRINCIPLE

The Vision Principle cannot be put in words any better than my golf coach used to say it—*If you can't see the shot, you can't hit the shot.*

If there is something you wish to do or become in your lifetime, create a plan for the accomplishment of that dream. Do not wait around foolishly believing that one day by some cosmic wave of events everything will be perfect, and your aspirations will achieve themselves. They won't.

God has endowed us all in so many different ways. Engage your talents and abilities.

—∿—

Plans and goals bring the most out of the human spirit.

Leaders, legends, heroes, champions, and saints are in the habit of constantly planning and setting goals. They never entertain the illusion that there will be no problems. When problems and challenges emerge they assess them and define them clearly and precisely. Then they create a plan to overcome or alleviate the problems. Thus, creating confidence and reducing fear.

If you have a problem, face it. If you don't, you empower the problem, and paralyze yourself with fear.

The Rhythm of Life provides an overall vision, but each area of our lives needs a specific vision.

Have a vision.

THE LIFE PRINCIPLE

As a teenager, and since, observing the lives of legends, heroes, champions, leaders, and saints, I discovered that just about every single one of them has or had, what I call, a Life Principle. A Life Principle is one sentence, phrase, or idea, that sums up the focus of a person's life. In the early 80's there was a popular film titled *Wall Street* starring Michael Douglas, Charlie Sheen, Martin Sheen, and Daryl Hannah. It was the story of Gordon Gecko, the biggest trader on Wall Street.

The movie reveals a trail of greed, lust, lying, cheating, using, and insider trading. Bud Fox, a rookie on Wall Street, hustles his way into Gordon Gecko's world, but not without paying a price. Gordon Gecko's Life Principle was—"Greed is good."

In the earlier part of this century a young woman from a very wealthy family left home to join a convent to live a life of poverty, chastity, and obedience. But before too long, she began to hear a voice within her calling her to something more. Within she felt an unquenchable concern for the poor and suffering of the world. It began simply as a desire. A healthy desire. A noble desire. A desire to help the poor. This young woman felt a need to serve her neighbor. She had a talent, simply to love and uphold the dignity of the poor.

In 1997 Mother Teresa died, leaving behind a legacy of love and service in almost every country around the world. She is an icon of compassion in our age. Mother Teresa's life principle was—"To care for the poorest of the poor."

Mother Teresa's Life Principle constantly challenged her to be a better person. Her Life Principle led her to fulfill her legitimate needs. She discovered a rhythm to life, lived in accord with that rhythm, and developed into an extraordinary human being.

Did Gordon Gecko's Life Principle lead him to be a better person?

People of ages to come may find it difficult to believe that one such as Mother Teresa ever walked the earth in flesh and blood. She was a hero, a teacher, a warrior, a prophet, a saint, a champion, a queen—and a tremendous success in her field. Mother Teresa is a legend.

The lives of successful people have direction. They do not react to the day-to-day happenings, but rather, their life is a conscious action, moving towards a specifically defined goal, directed by a carefully considered philosophy, which is summarized by a single principle—a Life Principle.

Their Life Principle brings them into focus, keeps them focused, and protects them from becoming distracted.

Everyday, hundreds of options exist for us to expend our time, effort, and energy. Dozens of opportunities emerge in the day-to-day happenings of our lives that distract us from what is really important. Successful people do not allow these distractions to take a grip of their lives. In each moment of decision throughout the day they carefully consider the opportunity before them in relation to their life principle. They constantly ask themselves, "Will this help me achieve my goal?" "Will this help me along the path towards *Point B*?" They use their life principle as their guide or navigator. It becomes the guiding principle of their lives and the anchor of their dreams.

For people who know what they want and where they are going the whole world will get out of the way.

—⁓—

As I explained earlier, until I was nineteen, my goal and ambition was simply to excel in the business world, to make a lot of money, and to enjoy the things of this world. But at nineteen, God touched my life in a special way, opening my eyes. It was at that time that I began to really reflect on life and the world in which we live. It was at that time that I first began to really pray and meditate.

Today, my Life Principle is this—*"What you become is infinitely more important than what you do or what you have."* This idea brings me to focus on change, growth, and development. It challenges me to dedicate my efforts and energies to those activities which will help me to become the better person I know I can be. When an opportunity emerges in my life I can simply weigh its worth by this one idea, this Life Principle, by asking myself these questions, "Will this opportunity help me to change, develop, and grow?" "Will I 'become' the better person through the pursuit of this opportunity?" "Will this opportunity help me to fulfill my legitimate needs?" "If I accept this opportunity will I be following my star?"

Without the direction and guidance that a Life Principle brings to our lives, we are like ships headed for shipwreck. Without a foundation principle we find ourselves in the dark and confusing abyss of deciding based upon "what we feel like" at any given moment. Our feelings are transitory and always changing. If we make our decisions based upon our ever changing feelings, our lives will have no theme, no rhythm, no continuity, and no consistency. We will lose the thread of our lives, we will lose our own personal story, and we will become insane. Quite literally.

We should develop the habit of viewing our current life questions in relation to a life principle.

Our Life Principle becomes the tool to bringing focus to our day. It is practical, it is effective, and the more we stay focused on this principle, the more we are able to attend to our legitimate physical, emotional, intellectual, and spiritual needs. The more we attend to these legitimate needs the more we are energized. This energy maximizes our capacity in each area of our lives. By planning our days according to our legitimate needs, with the guidance and direction of this Life Principle we know we are doing as much as we can without sacrificing the rhythm—and there is a certain peace and liberation that comes from that knowing.

All of these work together to create and form *The Rhythm of Life*. The rhythm annihilates restlessness by giving birth to balance, harmony, and peace. It is about knowing our limits and never exceeding them—for our own good. It begins by having a goal, a focus, a foundation, a Life Principle.

Take a blank sheet of regular letter size paper, and ask someone to hold it for you, horizontally, by the long ends. Now, try to punch a hole in it. You can't do it, can you?

Okay, now this time, take the same piece of paper, ask the other person to hold it exactly the same way, but instead of trying to punch a hole through it with your fist, poke a hole through the sheet of paper with your index finger. What happens? Your finger goes straight through, yes? FOCUS. Focus achieves results in our lives. That is why we need a Life Principle. It brings focus to our lives.

Crystallize your purpose. Work out what your Life Principle is going to be. Write it down in your own words. Adopt someone else's if it seems appropriate. Use mine if it works for you. But write it down, stick it on the wall next to your bed, write it in your planner, put it on the dash of your car, magic tape it to your wardrobe door, put it on your desk, your screen saver, wherever necessary. Put a copy of your Life Principle everywhere, until it becomes such a constant and habitual part of your daily thought patterns and processes that you no longer need the visual stimulation.

Remind yourself of your goal in every waking moment of every hour of every day—that's what successful people do. They dream the dream, define the dream, continually visualize the dream, and they achieve the dream.

Then live it. Allow your Life Principle to become the foundation of all activity in your life. Let it become your guide and advisor in times of decision, let it become your comforter and assurance in times of fear and doubt. Allow it to affect every decision and action of your day. Allow it to become your Life Principle—the foundation of all you are, all you do, all you have, and of all you are becoming.

Once you have decided upon your Life Principle you can test it by asking these questions: Does my Life Principle build me up and make me more fully and perfectly myself? Does my Life Principle enrich, ennoble, and empower me? Will it help me to become the better person I know I can be?

What you become is infinitely more important than what you do, or what you have.

—*ww*—

It doesn't interest me what you do for a living.

    I want to know what you ache for, and if you dare to dream of meeting your heart's longing.

It doesn't interest me how old you are.

    I want to know if you will risk looking like a fool for love, for your dreams, for the adventure of being alive.

It doesn't interest me what planets are squaring your moon.

    I want to know if you have touched the center of your own sorrow, if you have been opened by life's betrayals or have become shriveled and closed for fear of further pain. I want to know if you can sit with pain, mine or your own, without moving to hide it or fade it or fix it. I want to know if you can be with joy, mine or your own; if you can dance with wildness and let the ecstasy fill you to the tips of your fingers and toes without cautioning us to be careful, to be realistic, or to remember the limitations of being a human.

It doesn't interest me if the story you're telling me is true.

    I want to know if you can disappoint another to be true to yourself; if you can bear the accusation of betrayal and not betray your own soul. I want to know if you can be faithful and therefore be trustworthy. I want to know if you can see the beauty even when it is not pretty everyday, and if you can source your life from ITS presence. I want to know if you can live with failure, yours and mine, and still stand on the edge of a lake and shout to the silver of the full moon, "Yes!"

It doesn't interest me to know where you live or how much money you have.

I want to know if you can get up after a night of grief and despair, weary and bruised to the bone, and do what needs to be done for the children.

It doesn't interest me who you are, or how you came to be here.

I want to know if you will stand in the center of the fire with me and not shrink back.

It doesn't interest me where or what or with whom you have studied.

I want to know what sustains you from the inside when all else falls away. I want to know if you can be alone with yourself, and if you truly like the company you keep in the empty moments.

—Oriah Mountain Dreamer, Indian Elder

THE THOUGHT PRINCIPLE

In my late teenage years, as I began to reflect on some of the ideas I am now sharing with you, I searched for practical ways to center my lifestyle on my Life Principle. This question became my touchstone—"What will it take today for me to become the better person I know I can be?"

The first thing I did was write this question down on a blank piece of paper and stuck it on the wall next to my bed. I did this because I wanted this to be the first thing I saw each day. I wanted it to be the first thing I saw each day because I wanted it to become the theme of my day.

Have you ever woken up with a song in your head? What happens? You find yourself humming the song all day long. Even though you don't like the song, you can't get it out of your head. You find yourself humming the song all day. You hate the song, and yet you discover you know all the words to the song.

There is something very powerful about these first moments of the day. I don't know exactly why, but I know they are powerful. The wise thing to do would be to harness the power of that moment. That is why I stuck that question next to my bed.

Then, I wrote it down again, "What will it take today for me to become the better person I know I can be?" and I stuck it on the mirror in my bathroom. I wrote it down again and stuck it on my closet door—on my desk—on my planner—on the dash of my car—on my fridge... I put it everywhere. Why? Because I wanted to be reminded of my goal in every waking moment of every hour of every day. Why? Because that is how the legends, heroes, champions, leaders, and saints, achieved all they did.

I don't have those pieces of paper everywhere anymore, I just automatically think of that question—"What will it take today for me to become the better person I know I can be?"—3972 times every day. It has become a habit.

Human thought is creative. What you think, becomes. What you allow to occupy your mind forms the reality of your life and affects the whole world for generations to come. Thought determines action. Before too long you will be living out what has already happened in your mind. Good or bad, everything happens in your mind before it happens in reality. If you can control what happens in your mind, you can control every action of your life.

A basketball player steps up to the free-throw line. The scores are tied, there is one second left on the clock, it is three-three in the series, the NBA championship is at stake, and he has one shot. If he imagines himself missing the shot, what will he do? Of course, he will miss the shot. Thought determines action. If he imagines himself making the shot fifteen times and missing it nineteen times, what will he do? He will miss. The actions of our lives are determined by our last most dominant thought.

Your future is forged and your actions determined by your most dominant thoughts.

Jack Nicklaus didn't think only occasionally about being a great golfer—it was his most dominant thought for years. Cal Ripken Jr. doesn't think occasionally about being a great baseball player—it is his most dominant thought. Shakespeare didn't think occasionally about being a great writer—it was his most dominant thought. Michelangelo didn't think occasionally about being a great painter—it was his most dominant thought. Francis of Assisi didn't think occasionally about the wonder of God and His creation—it was his most dominant thought.

What is your most dominant thought? The answer to that question will tell you a lot about who you are and what you are doing with your life.

The Thought Principle is *Thought Determines Action*.

THE DEDICATION PRINCIPLE

Have you ever given your best, your all to anything? What do you think would happen if you did?

Love doesn't count the cost. Jack Nicklaus loves golf. Michael Jordan loves basketball. Mahatma Ghandi loved the people of India. Beethoven loved music. Michelangelo loved to paint. The legends, heroes, leaders, champions, and saints that fill our history books loved what they did. People of this caliber dedicate their whole being to their pursuits.

This is the Dedication Principle—*In order to love what you do, you must do what you love.*

THE BELIEF PRINCIPLE

The Belief Principle—*You were created for a purpose, and everything happens for a reason.*

This was Albert Einstein's reflection, *"There are two ways to live life. One is as though nothing is a miracle. The other is as though everything is a miracle."*

The choice is yours.

THE PEOPLE PRINCIPLE

I believe one of the greatest problems in relationships today is caused by a simple modern fallacy. In our age, understanding is posed as the foundation of relationship. It is not. The foundation of relationship is acceptance.

It is a great wisdom to accept people where they are on the journey. Acceptance is the welcoming open arms of relationship.

The People Principle is—*People Deserve to be Cherished.*

In order to cherish people we must look beyond our personal preferences, prejudices, and judgmental inclinations to discover and reverence the wonder and marvel of the individual.

It is helpful to remember that we are all at different points along the path. Our ability to love and cherish people increases infinitely as we learn to accept people for who they are and where they are on their own personal journey. Some people are at places we ourselves have been before, others are in places we have not yet been. It is a journey—trust that the same God who is moving you towards your purpose and dreams, is moving them towards theirs. Even when you cannot understand people, accept them, cherish them.

Along the way you will meet many people. Some of them you will help, assist, advise. Others will help, assist, and advise you. It has been my experience that when you think you are there to help someone else, chances are they are really there to help you. Our students make the best teachers.

Without the help of others you will never make the journey. It is simply part of the Divine plan that we make this journey together.

It is a funny thing I have observed about life—mistakes are almost always and inevitably one's own responsibility, but our successes, triumphs, and worthwhile achievements are very rarely posted without the help of others.

The greatest barrier to loving people, to cherishing people, and to accepting people is our inability to see ourselves in them. Take a closer look. We are one. To see ourselves in others, and others in ourselves—that is wisdom.

My father always told me that the key to success in business is personal relationships. My mother always told me that the key to a rich and rewarding personal life is personal relationships. I have discovered that the key to an abundant spiritual life is personal relationship.

Life is relationship. How are you relating? How are your relationships?

People are a gift. Each person that crosses through your life is a chance to love, a chance to really live. Cherish people.

THE COMMUNICATION PRINCIPLE

The Communication Principle is—*Be clear, concise, open, and honest.*

Communication is an art. I have seen some great communicators at work. These are some of the lessons I have learned.

Let others talk. Avoid arguments. Don't complain. Give honest and sincere compliments. Appreciate people. Always compliment more than you criticize. Compliment before you criticize. Invite input. Never be afraid to seek advice. Never criticize someone in front of other people. Be aware of other people's desires. Find joy and pleasure through taking an interest in people. Only talk about yourself if asked. Smile—it is contagious and opens people's hearts. Learn to listen. Remember other people's names, it is music to their ears. Remember people's birthdays and anniversaries—it shows you care. Encourage people to share about themselves. Engage people where they are—talk in relation to their interests. Help other people to discover their uniqueness, to feel special and important, without patronizing them. Respect other people's opinions. Admit when you are wrong. Be kind and friendly to every person you meet. Ask questions people respond to positively. Encourage other people in their dreams—particularly children. Try to see it from the other person's point of view. Hold up ideals. Challenge people gently. Talk about your own failures. Appeal to higher motives. Always look for yourself in others and others in yourself—it affirms the oneness of the human family. Affirm the highest values of the human spirit.

Be clear, concise, open, and honest.

THE FINAL PRINCIPLE

It is a long journey. Some make it and others fall by the wayside. We all love the beauty of the diamond, but we forget the time and pressure it took to make it. Along the way we become discouraged. It seems too hard. It isn't. It seems impossible. It isn't.

There will be set-backs and failures. Winners are inspired by failure. Losers are afraid of and discouraged by failure. In the wake of failure, winners want to do more, to be more, to do a better job next time. When faced with failure, losers become overwhelmed by the fear of greater failure. They allow that fear to smother them and in the process achieve what they wanted to avoid—a greater failure. The greatest failure is to not try.

There are always plenty of reasons to give up. Think of reasons not to give up, to stay strong, to stay focused, and to persevere.

Once you set yourself at something, keep your eye on your goal, and employ the Final Principle—*Never Give Up*!

—⁓—

If there ever was a tale of American leadership and perseverance, it is that of Abraham Lincoln.

Lincoln was born into poverty in 1809. Throughout his life he continually faced set-backs and defeats. He twice failed in business, lost eight elections, and suffered a nervous breakdown.

Defeat and failure were often beckoning him, inviting him to quit, but he refused that invitation and his story is one of extraordinary perseverance. This is a sketch of his life.

In 1816 Lincoln's family was forced out of their home and he had to go to work to support them. In 1818 his mother died. In 1831 he failed in business. In 1832 he ran for state legislature and lost. In 1832 he lost his job. That same year he decided he wanted to go to law school, but his application was rejected. In 1833 Lincoln borrowed some money from a friend to begin a business, but by the end of the year he was bankrupt. He spent the next seventeen years paying off that debt. In 1834 he ran for state legislature again and lost. In 1835 he was engaged to be married, but his fiancée died and it broke his heart. In 1836 Lincoln suffered a total nervous breakdown and was confined to his bed for six months. In 1838 he sought to become speaker of the State Legislature and was defeated. In 1840 he sought to become Elector and was defeated. In 1843 he ran for Congress and lost. In 1846 he ran for Congress again, this time he won and finally made his way to Washington. In 1848 Lincoln ran for reelection to Congress and lost. In 1849 he sought the job of Land Officer but was rejected. In 1854 he ran for Senate of the United States and lost. In 1856, he sought the vice-presidential nomination at his party's national convention. He got less than one hundred votes and lost. In 1858, he ran for the United States Senate again and lost again. Then, in 1860, Lincoln decided to run for President... I mean, based on what? His track record?

He won, and went on to become one the greatest presidents in the history of the United States, and one of the finest models of leadership in modern times. In a speech Lincoln said, *"The path was worn and slippery, my foot slipped from under me knocking the other foot out of the way—but I recovered, and said to myself—it's a slip, not a fall."*

—⚬⚬—

I've missed more than 9,000 shots in my career, I've lost more than 300 games, and 26 times I've been trusted to take the game winning shot and missed. Throughout my life and career I've failed, and failed, and failed again. And, that's why I succeed.

—Michael Jordan

THE TEN CHARACTER PRINCIPLES

Ten principles. Does Michael Jordan, Jack Nicklaus, and Cal Ripken Jr. employ these principles? Yes, absolutely. Did Shakespeare, Beethoven, and Michelangelo employ these principles? Yes, without a doubt. Did Francis of Assisi and Mother Teresa employ these principles? Yes, unquestionably.

Did their success manifest in different ways? Of course. Were their achievements each unique and different? They were. But the principles that we find at the core of their success are the same.

CHAPTER 7

THE ABUNDANT LIFE

ENJOY THE JOURNEY

One of our greatest failings as human beings is our inability to be present in our own lives. It may sound absurd, but it is true. Let me explain. How often do you find yourself in the company of a person, even in the middle of a conversation with a person, and yet thinking about other people and places? Often, we are distracted by the past and the future. Those distractions rob us of our lives. The past is history. The future is a mirage. The past was the present, the future will be the present. The only reality is now.

The other way this failing manifests itself is in our tendency to put off important matters. We tell ourselves, "When I get that promotion, I will spend more time with my wife and children," or "I will exercise next week, when I have this project out of the way."

Each activity has its own priority and place in our lives, whether it be work, prayer, leisure, exercise, or friendship. *The Rhythm of Life* helps us to give each activity its own place—everyday—and immerses us in the abundant life.

Over and over I have watched interviewers ask famous and successful people, "What would you change if you could do it all again?" So many of them reply by saying they would enjoy their rise to fame and success a little more if they had another chance. But you never hear them say, "I would work harder and spend less time with my family and friends."

Just last year I saw an interview with Billy Graham. The interview concentrated mostly on the works and achievements of his life, but towards the end the interviewer asked, "What would you do differently if you had to do it again?"

The change that came over Billy Graham's features I have never seen before. The interviewer had asked one of those questions that I suppose all interviewers dream of asking. A question that invites the host and his audience into the deepest recesses of the guest's heart. It was as though a veil had been torn. The expression on his face was one of knowing and it lingered there for a long moment. He paused, not to think how to answer, but to pull himself together. It was obvious he had asked himself the same question before. He looked down, swallowed, then looked back up again, and said, "I would spend more time with my family."

—〜〜—

Life is a journey. Enjoy the journey. Whether you are setting out to become a legend, a hero, a champion, a star, a leader, or a saint—enjoy the journey. If you do not enjoy life, you will be no good to anybody. The destination, the victory, the achievement—these only last a moment, and then they fade like the morning dew from the grass into little more than pleasant memories.

Success is not a destination—it is a journey.

Another of my favorite songwriters, James Taylor once wrote, *"The secret of life is enjoying the passing of time."* The joy is not in the destination, the joy is in the journey. If you cannot find peace in the journey, you will not find peace in the destination. Our passion, enthusiasm, and excitement should be for the journey. Don't put off important things using a destination, or an achievement, as an excuse. Take it easy. Slow and steady. Let things have their place.

Be present in your own life. It is an amazing and rare gift. When you meet a person who has this gift, there is no mistaking it. People who are present to their own lives have this striking ability to focus on who and what is before them. They give the people and the matters at hand their complete and undivided attention. When you stand before such a person in conversation he is able to make you feel as if no one else exists. It is just you and him. The noise around you, the people around you, even in rush hour on Madison Avenue, do not take even a breath of his attention from you and the conversation. For those few moments it is as if nothing else exists. For those few moments you are his life. To give his attention to anything else would be to miss something of his own life. Often we do.

Robert Hastings sums it up perfectly in his story *The Station*. Let me share it with you—

Tucked away in our subconscious is an idyllic vision. We see ourselves on a long trip that spans the continent. We are traveling by train. Out the windows we drink in the passing scenes of cars on nearby highways, or children waving at a crossing, or cattle grazing on a distant hillside, or smoke pouring from a power plant, or row upon row of corn and wheat, of flatlands and valleys, or mountains and rolling hillsides, or city skylines and village halls.

But uppermost in our minds is the final destination. On a certain day at a certain hour we will pull into the station. Bands will be playing and flags waving. Once we get there so many wonderful dreams will come true and the pieces of our lives will fit together like a completed jigsaw puzzle. How restlessly we pace the aisles, damning the minutes for loitering—waiting, waiting, waiting for the station.

"When we reach the station, that will be it!" we cry. "When I am 18." "When I buy my new 450SL Mercedes Benz!" "When I put the last kid through college." "When I get a promotion." "When I reach the age of retirement, I shall live happily ever after!"

Sooner or later we must realize there is no station, no one place to arrive at once and for all. The true joy of life is the trip. The station is only an illusion. It constantly outdistances us.

"Relish the moment" is a good motto. Especially when coupled with Psalm 118:24 "This is the day which the Lord has made; let us rejoice and be glad in it." It isn't the burdens of today that drive men mad. It is the regrets over yesterday and the fear of tomorrow. Regret and fear are twin thieves who rob us of today.

So stop pacing the aisles and counting the miles. Instead, climb more mountains, eat more ice cream, go barefoot more often, swim more rivers, watch more sunsets, laugh more, cry less. Life must be lived as we go along. The station will come soon enough.

MAKING A DIFFERENCE

What do all great men and women in history have in common? What raises a person beyond success, achievement, and excellence to the realm of greatness? Greatness is attained beyond the pursuit of our own fulfillment. Greatness is achieved by making a difference in other people's lives.

History is full of examples of great men and women, but we must be careful not to confuse greatness with fame or fortune. Fame and fortune are external qualities of a person's life. Greatness is an internal quality of a person's character, which emerges in his or her actions.

Some examples that readily come to mind are people like Ghandi, Helen Keller, Martin Luther King, Mother Teresa, and Jesus. But most of the people who have developed and mastered this greatness of which we speak are not public figures or celebrities. They are mothers and fathers, teachers and doctors, preachers, rabbis, ministers, priests... They are people from all walks of life who turn their talents, efforts, and energies towards the uplifting of other people. They make a difference in other people's lives. When you meet such a person you see a certain calm in her eyes and she seems to be unusually happy. She is quietly confident and occupied with a serene satisfaction.

There is no greater satisfaction than laying your head on the pillow at night and knowing you have touched another person's life, made their burden lighter, taught them some infinite wisdom, made them laugh, allowed them to cry on your shoulder, lent them an understanding ear... made a difference.

One of my favorite childhood movies was *Willy Wonka and the Chocolate Factory*. It is the story of Mr. Wonka, the most successful and famous candy maker in the world, and his search to find someone to continue his work when he is gone. Wonka places five golden tickets randomly inside candy bars and announces a contest. Each person who finds a golden ticket will win a one day tour of Wonka's Chocolate Factory—which no one has been inside for twenty years—and a lifetime supply of chocolate.

Charlie, the child of a single mother in England, dreams, wishes, prays, and hopes, that he will find one of the five golden tickets. But his family is desperately poor and he has no money to buy chocolate bars. One day on his way home from school Charlie finds some money in the street, buys two Wonka Bars, and finds the fifth and final golden ticket.

The next day Charlie and four other children from around the world, each with a companion of their choice, enter into the mysterious and magical world of Willy

Wonka's Chocolate Factory. Charlie asks his Grandpa Joe to go with him, and they set off on an adventure to live out Charlie's wildest dream.

The other four golden ticket winners are fatally flawed with large doses of selfishness, and one by one they find themselves leaving the tour of the factory prematurely. But Charlie is gentle, kind, and thoughtful.

Wonka takes them from one wonderful exhibition to another, showing them all the wonders of his candy-making genius and imagination. Before long it is just Charlie, Grandpa Joe, and Wonka left on the tour—but as they come out of the Wonka-Vision Studio, Mr. Wonka's tone and mood change dramatically. He bids Charlie and his grandfather farewell and asks them to show themselves out. And with that, Wonka disappears into his office.

Standing at the office door Charlie looks at Grandpa Joe. Dumbfounded he says, "What happened? Did we do something wrong?" "I don't know, but I'm gonna find out," Grandpa Joe replies as he storms into Wonka's office.

Wonka's office is just as magical as any other room in the factory. Everything is in halves—half a desk, half a clock, half a picture, half a statue, half a mirror... Grandpa Joe says to Wonka who is sitting at his desk writing a letter, "What about the chocolate? The life-time supply of chocolate for Charlie!" "He doesn't get any," Wonka spitefully replies.

Mr. Wonka appears to become quite angry and begins to explain that Charlie gets no chocolate. He goes to the filing cabinet and takes out half a photocopy of the contract Charlie and the other children had signed at the beginning of the tour, and half a magnifying glass. Wonka yells at Grandpa Joe, explaining that because they drank fizzy lifting drinks they had violated the contract, and that Charlie was no longer eligible for the lifetime supply of chocolate. "You're a crook, a cheat, a swindler," accuses Grandpa Joe as he turns to leave.

This is where the plot thickens. In Charlie's pocket is one Everlasting Gobstopper which Wonka had given him during the tour. It is the very Gobstopper Wonka's rival, Mr. Slugworth, had asked Charlie to get for him in exchange for more money than he could earn in ten lifetimes.

As they leave the office Grandpa Joe says to Charlie, "If Slugworth wants an Everlasting Gobstopper, that's just what he'll get."

With that, Charlie stops, takes Grandpa Joe's hand off his arm, turns around, and walks back into the office where Wonka is still sitting at his desk writing. From his pocket, Charlie takes the Everlasting Gobstopper and says, "Mr. Wonka!" as he places it on the desk. Without another word, he turns around and begins to walk slowly from the office.

Wonka doesn't look up, and he doesn't look at the Everlasting Gobstopper. He doesn't have to. He knows without looking. He just reaches across the desk and grasps the Gobstopper and whispers gently, *"And so shines a good deed in a weary world."*

With great excitement, Wonka swings around, calls Charlie back, and explains that it was a test to see if he would betray his promise never to show the Ever-Lasting-Gobstopper to anyone—and that Charlie had passed, and won, and that now he is going to give Charlie the Chocolate Factory.

I cannot describe to you the joy I felt as a child each time Charlie took the Everlasting Gobstopper from his pocket and placed it on the desk. I feel the same joy even today when I watch the movie. It is intense, it is exhilarating. His innocence I suppose, his honesty, his sincerity and integrity—all symbols of hope for a weary world.

"And so shines a good deed in a weary world." This is what our world needs. It is what we need. It is what makes the world a joy to live in. It is what fills us with a tangible sense of our own worth and wealth.

Our every action is an opportunity to carry the torch of hope to an often weary world. Each day is filled with endless possibilities to make a difference. It doesn't take much, for it really is a weary world for so many people. It is a world full of people desperately hungry for sincerity, honesty, and goodness. Most of them are men and women just like you and me. They don't have the power to change the world single handedly, so they think change must be someone else's responsibility. The truth is, no one has the power to change the world single handedly, but each of us has the power to make a difference.

Ideas change the world. Good ideas change it for the better. Bad ideas change it for the worse. Men and women share their ideas through their words and actions. What ideas are you sharing with the world?

Charlie shared the idea that honesty, integrity, and goodness are more important to a person's happiness than money. As a child I watched that movie and I wanted to be like Charlie. In my childhood I didn't understand it as I do now. That didn't matter. I knew that his deed was good and true, and I wanted to be like Charlie, and that was enough. Through his action Charlie shared his idea—and ideas are contagious.

Ideas change the world of today and form the world of tomorrow.

Make a difference. It is not that hard. Make a habit of making another person's day. Everyday.

Have you ever received an unexpected letter? I love to receive letters and I am fortunate to receive many, every day from people all around the world. They come from family and close friends, and also from people whom I have never met. It's a wonderful feeling to receive an unexpected letter—the excitement teetering on impatience as you open the envelope. Yet for most people it is a rare joy.

Do you remember the last time you received an unexpected letter? It was a wonderful experience, wasn't it? Do you remember the feeling? Did it make your day?

Write one. Write an unexpected letter today. Write a letter to an old friend whom you haven't seen in years, or to someone you love who you haven't written to in a while. It isn't that hard; it doesn't take that much. Write a short note on a small piece of paper, put it in an envelope, address the envelope, and take it down to your post office. It will cost you thirty-three cents and just a little of your time to make someone's day.

Or, when was the last time you bought someone a box of chocolates or a bunch of flowers? Not because it's their birthday or anniversary, or for any reason other than to brighten up their day. When was the last time you baked someone some chocolate chip cookies?

When was the last time you sat down the people you love and told them of your love for them? It's best to express it in your actions, but it doesn't hurt to say it. Perhaps you are married. When was the last time you told your spouse how much he or she means to you? When was the last time you sat your husband or wife down and said, "You know, for me, you are sun, rain, fire, ice, New York, LA, and every town along the way..."? It doesn't take that much, but it makes a difference.

Whisper, "I love you" in your sleeping child's ear.

These things may seem simple and external, but they reflect a much deeper quality in a person. Spiritually we strive to be patient because God is patient, we seek to be kind because God is kind, we try to be humble and gentle because they are the ways of God, we seek to love and be loved because God is love.

And yet, above everything else, beyond everything else, before everything else, after everything else, and during everything else—God is a giver. God always gives. He never takes. He only gives. Always giving. Giving is God's life and existence. For God giving is the perpetual motion of His being. That is why to give a box of chocolates, or a bunch of flowers, or to take time to write a letter is an act of greatness. It is an act of greatness because it is an act which emerges from the heart and mind of God. If all our actions could be performed with this disposition, we would be living "life to the fullest."

I promise you with absolute certitude there is no faster, surer way to share in the life, the power, and the infinite joy of God than to give. Give of your time, give of your talents, give of your resources to make a difference in other people's lives. It is the way of greatness. This is the way of God. It is the way of legends, heroes, stars, champions, leaders, and saints. I hope and pray that it becomes your way, and mine.

As a child, my father used to tell me, *"Whatever you give to another will return to you ten times."* Like so many things my father said to me, life has taught me that it is a wise and true statement. Another saying I recall from my childhood is, *"You get what you give."* When you refuse to give, holding on tightly to everything you have, you live in the realm of lack and limitation. When you give, you perform a significant and vital attitude change. By giving you express abundance—and what you express in thought, word, and action will become the reality of your life. Here, mysteriously veiled by the act of giving, we discover the abundant life.

When you give to assist in someone else's need, you learn very quickly that the satisfaction of giving is greater than the satisfaction of having.

As time goes by you realize that many of the things you once thought you needed, you don't really need. With this realization of your own abundance you are able to give more. Have you noticed that although God is always giving, He is never without? God is not lack, or limitation—God is abundance. For God, giving is like breathing—let it become so for you and for me and our lives will be full of excitement, passion, satisfaction, contentment, and fulfillment.

Otherwise we will become like the monkey who realized one day that his master had left the lid off the peanut jar. The monkey waited for his master to leave the house for his afternoon walk. When the master left, the monkey jumped up onto the table where the jar was, only to realize that the jar was only half full and too tall for him to reach the peanuts. The monkey knocked the jar over, but none of the peanuts fell out. So he reached into the jar and grabbed a large handful of peanuts and his eyes lit up. But as he went to take his hand out of the jar, he realized his hand wouldn't fit through the mouth of the jar while it was full of peanuts. The monkey looked at the peanuts and pulled harder and harder to no avail. He could see the peanuts, hold the peanuts, but couldn't enjoy them. Torture.

When the master returned, the monkey was still on the table clenching the handful of peanuts, refusing to let go. Foolish monkey.

Finding our place in the world, finding our place in our local community, and making a difference in our own way, gives meaning, purpose, and a deep, deep, sense of fulfillment to our lives. We must find it not only for ourselves, but help every individual to find the same.

—*\\//*—

The enemies of making a difference are doubt, fear, discouragement, and selfishness. Some people never try to make a difference because they doubt whether they can. Some people fear to try in case they fail. Some people start to make a difference, but compare the good they are doing with all the evil they can imagine in the world, and become disabled by discouragement. Some people are so absorbed in themselves that they never think of anyone's needs but their own.

On the other hand, some people trust that they were put here on this earth to make a difference in some way, large or small. Those same people know the fear of failure as much as any other, but they face that fear, immerse themselves in that emotion, and bravely move forward. They fight off discouragement by keeping things in perspective. When things get tough they take life just one day at a time. When things get really tough, they take life one hour at a time. And when things get unbearably difficult—they take heart, hold firm, and take life moment by moment. One by one. Little by little. They are not strangers to doubt, fear, discouragement, or selfish desires, but they find a focus in their lives and commit to that focus.

By now you are aware of my great love for stories. Parables, fables, and stories, are the most effective and powerful way to convey any idea or message. Here is a story that I would like you to recall when doubt, fear, discouragement, and selfish desires attempt to steal you away from your life's work of making a difference.

—∿∿—

Once upon a time there was a young boy who lived just near a beach. Every afternoon the boy would walk along the beach.

One day as he was walking he noticed that as the tide had gone out it had left many starfish stranded on the beach. He realized that if the starfish were left there they would die before the water returned. So as he walked along the beach, one by one he picked up the starfish and threw them back into the water. He couldn't pick them all up because there were too many, but the ones he could pick up he did.

From that day on, the boy would spend his afternoons walking along the beach throwing the starfish back into the water. Then one day as the boy was walking, an old man came walking in the other direction. The old man saw what the young boy was doing and cried out, "What are you doing, boy? You'll never make a difference. Why don't you just enjoy your walk?" The boy ignored the old man and continued to pick up the starfish, one by one, and to throw them back into the water. But as the old man got closer to the boy, he came right up to the boy and said, "What are you doing? What are you doing, boy? You'll never make a difference. Why don't you just enjoy your walk?"

The boy just stood there and said nothing. Then the old man grabbed the young boy by the arm, turned him around, and made him face down the beach. As the young boy and the old man looked down the beach they could see that there were many, many starfish. The old man said, "Look boy, there's hundreds of them, there's thousands of them. Look how many you have missed. You'll never make a difference. Forget about them. Just enjoy your walk."

Just then, the young boy bent down and reached into the sand one more time and picked up one more starfish. And standing up, he threw the starfish as far as he could into the ocean. Then looking deep into the old man's eyes he said, "I made a difference for that one."

—⁓—

There are four simple steps which will empower you to make a difference in other people's lives, and lead you along the path of greatness.

Step One. When you wake up tomorrow morning, the first thing I would like you to do is to remind yourself of your goal, your *Point B*, which by now you should have written down. *Step Two.* Then ask yourself, "Who's day can I make today?" *Step Three.* Now ask yourself, "How can I make that person's day?" *Step Four.* When you have made these first three steps, shower and have breakfast, but then, just before racing into the day, take a few minutes to plan, reflect, and pray. Find a quiet place, and in that silence visualize how you would like your day to unfold. Make plans to fulfill your legitimate needs physically, emotionally, intellectually, and spiritually. Take a moment to become aware of, and to appreciate all you have and all you are, and then you will be ready for the day.

If you faithfully commit yourself to this simple four step plan of action for the next ten days, your life will begin to be filled with the fruits of *The Rhythm of Life*—peace, joy, an increased ability to love, an increased ability to be loved, a rare happiness and satisfaction, a profound sense of fulfillment, and the love, excitement, and passion for life which are the essence of God, the essence of the human being, and the intended essence of the human experience.

You will then find yourself on the verge of greatness. You will have discovered the power of making a difference, and life will issue you the challenge to continually and consistently engage that power in your daily life.

After a while, you learn that it's better to write an unexpected letter than to sit around waiting for the postman to deliver one. Sooner or later, you discover that it is better to help someone plant a garden than to wait for someone to bring you flowers. Let it be sooner for you.

The temptation is to say, "I am just one person, what can one person do?" Look at what other men and women have done in just one lifetime: Billy Graham, Mother Teresa, Beethoven, Michelangelo, Frank Lloyd Wright, Albert Einstein, Michael Jordan, Steven Spielberg, Bill Gates, Abraham Lincoln. They too could have used the same excuse, "I am only one person." They didn't. But rather, they dedicated themselves to the passionate pursuit of their dreams. Theodore Roosevelt offers us a starting point, *"Do what you can, with what you have, where you are."* Francis of Assisi offered this advice to his brothers, *"First do what is necessary, then what is possible, and before long you will be doing the impossible."*

The good we do is never lost, it never dies. In other people, in other places, in other times—the good we do lives on forever. Do good.

Be the difference that makes the difference.

LEADERS, CRITICS, DREAMERS, AND THE FUTURE

We are living during a very interesting period of history, a time of transition. Transition periods are the most important, and yet, you rarely read about them in history books, because it's difficult to judge exactly when they begin and when they end. They lie subtly sandwiched between other periods in history. We are living in such a transition period now, but in order to understand this time in which we live, and particularly this transition, we must first try to understand what is on either side of this transition.

The reality is that our civilization is in decline. There are five signs that emerge in a declining civilization. These signs can be found in the decline of almost every civilization in recorded history. They take different forms depending on the culture of the people of the time and the technological advancement of the age, but ultimately the same devastating result is achieved.

These are the five signs of a declining civilization: a dramatic increase in sexual promiscuity; the political undermining and disintegration of family values; the cultural destruction of the family unit; the killing of the innocent; and a radical increase in non-warfare violence. These signs have played a major role in the decline and collapse of every civilization in recorded history. So much so, that once these signs have emerged to some level of general occurrence and acceptance, no civilization has been able to prolong its existence for longer than one hundred years.

In our own culture these signs gained initial prominence during and after World War I. They were compounded and spread even more widely by the effects and consequences of World War II, and by the end of the 1960's they were rampant. At the turn of the millennium they have all but been generally accepted as valid views and forms of behavior. Therefore, using a date even as late as the 1960's as the landmark for the general emergence of these signs, our civilization is left with only sixty years. This is not a prediction, it is not a prophecy, just a reality set in the past. It is a lesson we have continually failed to learn from history. And, sixty years is a short time for one person, never mind a civilization.

When present generations ignore the past, they destine themselves to relive the mistakes and miseries of every age.

We live in a critical time in history. The future of humanity and the world is in danger unless radical change is adopted. This change must focus not primarily on the external realities of the world, but on the interior mysteries of our being. God is not going to destroy humanity, nor is God going to bring the world to an end. But, collectively and progressively we have involved ourselves in a complex process of self-destruction, and so have endangered the world and all creation.

This process of self-destruction gathers its force and momentum in the ideology that anything and everything can be exploited and consumed for profit and our own satisfaction. The result is disorder. The disorder begins with misplaced priorities in our hearts, and leads to disorder socially, politically, culturally, economically, environmentally, and spiritually. This produces chaos and destruction—gradual at first, but escalating.

What does all this mean? Is the world going to end? No. Is humanity going to be completely wiped out? No. We are passing from one time to another. One civilization is dying and another will emerge. We are in a transition.

To understand this a little more we should turn to our history books to learn another lesson. There is, I believe, a remarkable parallel between the time in which we live and the later years of the Roman Empire. The Roman Empire was great. It was mighty. It was powerful. And the people of that time believed that the Roman Empire would continue ruling and conquering, and enjoying the fruits of ruling and conquering forever. There came a time, however, when some of the people began to realize that the Roman Empire, even as great and as powerful as it was, would not last forever. The sages and the seers of that era perceived that the Empire was in decline, and that before too long it would give way to something new.

A very similar progression now awaits on the doorstep of human history. The 'Modern Western Empire' has reached that point. It has achieved it's pinnacle. It may linger there at the top momentarily, but not for long. Today's climate makes Nero's Rome look like the Mad-Hatter's Tea Party. The people of our age, just like the people of the Roman Empire, believe that the Modern Western Empire will continue ruling and conquering forever, and that forever we will go on enjoying the fruits of our ruling and conquering. Like most things, it cannot last forever, and soon will begin to fall away, making way for something new.

History also teaches us that the Roman Empire gave way to a wonderful period in history—the Middle Ages. Culturally, socially, politically, economically, and spiritually, the Middle Ages were a vibrant and vital time of growth, discovery, and progress. I am not suggesting that we go back to the Middle Ages. I am suggesting that on the other side of this present transition is potentially a time unmatched by any other in history.

There is one question that the people of any age are always asking, whether consciously or subconsciously, "What will the future hold?"

The Twentieth Century has been marked by tremendous advancement in the material and scientific realms. Six hundred years passed between the invention of the plough and the invention of the automobile. It took only sixty years from the invention of the automobile to the space age. This single fact alone helps us to understand the confusion that has also marked the Twentieth Century. This rapid change has challenged people to reassess their view of reality. The results have not always been positive or progressive. Perhaps because of this rapid change alone, and the associated confusion, we now find ourselves preparing to be catapulted into a new period in history.

The Twenty-first Century will not be marked by rapid increases in technology, but by dramatic and radical increases in people's awareness of the transcendental, a growing understanding of the vital role spirituality plays in our existence, and the importance of tending to all of humanity's legitimate needs.

To whom then does the future belong? If we look closely at other transition periods in history, there are two groups of people that emerge very strongly. The first are what we know as critics—people who criticize. Critics exist in any period, of course, but in a time of transition they multiply faster than ever. What do they criticize? They criticize the old, they criticize the new, they criticize the change, they criticize the change for being too fast, and they criticize the change for being too slow. They criticize everything and anything. A critic is never hard to find. The questions we should consider are: When did a group of critics ever usher in a new movement in history? Never. When will a group of critics ever usher in a new movement in history? Never.

So to whom does the future belong?

The second group of people that a transition raises are leaders. They are men and women of vision, courage, persistence, confidence, generosity, conscience, integrity, creativity, enthusiasm, character, and virtue. They have the extraordinary ability to ignore the chaos, confusion, troubles, and difficulties that surround them and to remain focused on the task at hand. They have the awe-inspiring and profound ability to pierce through time into the future and envision how they wish, think, or believe, the future should be. Then they return to the here and now and work tirelessly to make their vision a reality. They are able to share their vision and muster support from others for that vision. They are extraordinary communicators both in word and deed, and their mere presence energizes and inspires people. Against all odds, doubts, and criticisms they are able to trust, follow, nurture, and share the goodness within them.

The future belongs to such people as these. They are leaders. You rarely hear them criticizing anything or anyone, because they are too busy getting the job done, ushering in a new movement in history.

They say the darkest hour is right before the dawn. But the darkest hour gives birth to the greatest children of light. From the dark hours of history are born legends, heroes, champions, prophets, sages, leaders, stars, great teachers, and saints.

The future will be what we make of it. Leadership is not an elite class. It is a role each of us are born into. It is a position of influence. Granted, some people exert more influence than others, but all of us exert some, and by our influence, people's lives are touched. People hear what you say, and they listen, and they are affected. People watch how you live, and they learn, and they are influenced.

Be a leader. Do not be afraid. Do not internalize the proclamations and criticisms of the "timid souls" and self-appointed kings of non-existent kingdoms. When you speak to yourself, let your interior dialogue be confident, optimistic, and visionary. Dare to live the life most people only fanaticize about. Do not be a destroyer of dreams, be a dreamer of dreams. Along the way, think often of Albert Einstein's words, *"Great spirits have always encountered violent opposition from mediocre minds."*

Life is not a popularity contest.

Those who wish to be free from criticism inevitably end up doing nothing worthwhile. I am often criticized. It is not something I will ever become accustomed to, and it drains tremendous energy from me if I am not careful. In the face of criticism I like to spend my Sacred Hour carefully reflecting on the following two quotes.

I do the very best I know how—the best I can; and I mean to keep doing so until the end. If the end brings me out all right, what is said against me won't amount to anything. If the end brings me out wrong, ten angels swearing I was right would make no difference.
—Abraham Lincoln

It is not the critic that counts; nor the man who points out how the strong man stumbled or where the doer of deeds could have done them better. The credit belongs to the man who is actually in the arena; whose face is marred by dust and sweat and blood; who strives valiantly; who errs, and comes short again and again, because there is no effort without error and shortcomings, who does actually try to do the deed; who knows the great enthusiasm, the great devotion, and spends himself in a worthy cause; who, at worst, if he fails, at least fails while daring greatly.

Far better it is to dare mighty things, to win glorious triumphs even though checkered by failure, than to rank among those timid souls who neither enjoy nor suffer much, because they live in the gray twilight that knows neither victory nor defeat.
—Theodore Roosevelt

Any society or community at any time in history needs leadership. Our age is no different, and perhaps more in need than any other age. The need is for authentic leadership—in our families, in our communities, in the business world, on the sporting field, in the areas of the arts and culture, in politics, and in our churches.

One thing is certain. In a land where there are no musicians; in a land where there are no storytellers, teachers, and poets; in a land where there are no men and women of vision and leadership; in a land where there are no legends, saints, and champions; in a land where there are no dreamers—the people of that land will most certainly perish. But, you and I, we are the music makers; we are the storytellers, teachers, and poets; we are the men and women of vision and leadership; we are the legends, the saints, and the champions; and, we are the dreamers of the dreams.

HOW DO YOU PERCEIVE THE WORLD?

How do you see the world? What is your perception of the world? The great danger is to fall into the trap of believing that the whole world is like the city we live in. The temptation is to fall into the subconscious lethargy of thinking that the whole world is like the street we live on.

If the world's population were proportionally reduced to one hundred people, there would be fifty-seven Asians, twenty-one Europeans, fourteen people from North and South America, and eight Africans. Fifty-one would be women, forty-nine men. Seventy would be non-Christian, thirty Christian. More than half of the world's wealth would belong to just six people, all of those six would be U.S. citizens. Sixty-eight of the one hundred would be unable to read or write. One would be near death, one would be just born, and only one would have been to college. By the turn of the millennium, fifty percent of children in the US will live separated from their biological fathers. One-third of the world is dying from lack of bread. One-third of the world is dying from lack of justice. And one-third of the world is dying from over-eating.

What is your view of the world? How do you perceive the world?

The way I see it is, life comes down to two simple realities. People were made to be loved, and things were made to be used. Your problems, my problems, and indeed all the world's problems come from our misunderstanding of these two simple principles—you see, we love things and we use people. It would not be too much to dedicate one's whole life to the reversal of these simple realities.

Love is our greatest desire—to love and be loved. We know how to love, because we know how we wish to be loved. It is the central precept and principle of every major religion. It is the answer to every question. It is the solution to every problem.

The answer is never to love less. The answer is always to love more.

The question is, "What do we love?"

You can chose not to love the right things, but you cannot chose not to love. We all love—we cannot help but love, for that is what we were created for. Love is what gives meaning to our lives. Love is the direction of our lives. What you love and what captivates your imagination determines how you live your life. Love is our greatest desire, our greatest need, our greatest talent, and our greatest yearning. Love is our identity.

Until we love, we never truly know who we are. Love is natural, original, and spontaneous. Love is power. I once heard it said, *"If you could only love enough, you could be the most powerful person in the world."*

We hold back that infinite power to love because when it is released—although it achieves all the good in the world—it also makes us vulnerable and ushers in the possibility of suffering. We waste opportunities to love.

In order to love deeply, you must let go of those illusions of perfection, that pretense of being completely in control, and open yourself to that mysterious gift, pleasure, power, and grace we call love. That surrender and openness creates a radical vulnerability. Love is to step beyond the comfort zone.

My mother has always enjoyed her garden, but particularly growing orchids. Mum has grown them in our backyard ever since I was a child. When my brothers and I were younger we used to play a lot of soccer and cricket in the backyard. One of us was always crawling toward the kitchen to confess the accidental assassination of one of Mum's orchids.

I overheard a conversation one night between my mother and father. My mother was venting that we were killing all her orchids. My father listened and a little time passed before he calmly said, "Well, one day they won't be here to play in the yard and break the orchids. When that day comes we will wish they were, so, let's move the plants."

The people you love will not always be near you. Love them. Seize the opportunity.

The most wonderful thing about love is that it is highly contagious. Love demands a response. Love determines the response. Love begets love. Here's a simple example—if you're walking down the street and your eyes meet with someone coming in the opposite direction, what happens? Usually they smile back. But in the event that they do not smile back, and the next day you see them again, and smile again, then what happens? Eventually they smile back. Love demands a response. Your love sets off a reaction, a ripple effect. Love begets love.

Tielhard de Chardin wrote, *"The day will come when, after harnessing space, the winds, the tides and gravitation, we shall harness for God the energies of love. And on that day, for the second time in the history of the world, we shall have discovered fire."*

If you have bought into the modern definition of success—"getting what you want out of life"—you have probably alienated yourself from the most important reality and truth of life. Love is a free gift.

We sacrifice love for so-called progress. We sacrifice love for so-called success. We sacrifice love for so-called more important things—no such things exist.

Tell me what you love and I will tell you who you are. What you fall in love with determines everything.

Our desire to love and be loved never rests. Though we may sleep, our desire to love never does. It is as constant as our very breathing—and as necessary. Our true identity is deeply intertwined with this desire and ability to love.

We cannot live without love. Without love there is no joy, excitement, passion, or satisfaction in life. You cannot live without love for yourself. You cannot live without love for your God. You cannot live without love for your neighbor. You can try, but you will end up bitter and miserable. And that bitterness and the misery will kill you in the end. You will appear to be alive, but in truth you will be dying. You cannot live without love.

Love or perish, there is no other alternative.

CAN YOU HEAR THE MUSIC?

For me, one of the greatest joys in this world is music. Can you imagine a world without music? What a weary, weary world that would be. Music is expressive of every human feeling and emotion, but it most aptly expresses joy and love. What holds music together? Rhythm.

What holds our lives together? Rhythm. Is your world a world without music? Is your life a song without rhythm?

Rests and pauses are as important in great music as the notes themselves. Rests and pauses are as important in great lives as activity.

—◦◦◦—

It is natural for us to want a better world for our children to grow up in. We must recognize that to achieve great change for the common good takes a long time. Those working for good are not in a hurry. They are patient, and because they are patient, they are wise. They do all they can to bring on this good without losing *The Rhythm of Life* themselves. They never sacrifice the rhythm.

You must find the rhythm, *your* rhythm. The rhythm that connects you with the rest of creation in harmony and peace. The rhythm that most effectively allows the grace of God to work within your life. The rhythm that allows you to find that sacred balance that gives you strength, courage, and confidence to be yourself. The rhythm that leads you along the path of growth and perfection. *The Rhythm of Life* which unveils and fulfills your legitimate needs.

The Rhythm of Life is a powerful thing.

In Chapter One I suggested that any adequate solutions to the problems and challenges that face us in the world today must be both accessible and applicable to everyone, everywhere, regardless of age, color, creed, or culture—and their practicality must impact and be deeply intertwined with people's day-to-day living. I believe *The Rhythm of Life* offers such a solution.

Let me issue one warning. *The Rhythm of Life* may be the solution to many of the world's problems, but in this day and age—in a world obsessed with speed, noise, greed, lust, and activity—*The Rhythm of Life* is a radical counter-cultural revolutionary act.

—ᴡᴡ—

If you decide to walk the path I have described in this book, not everyone will understand. Some of your family and friends will ridicule you, they will accuse you of being a dreamer, they will tell you you are crazy.

The people who cannot hear the music think that the people who are dancing are crazy.

Don't let that bother you. And even if it does bother you, don't let it discourage or distract you from walking the path. If they understood the path they would be on it. Some of them are bitter because once in their youth they tried to walk this path and gave up, and now in their old age they believe it is too late for them to seek that path again. This path is not for everyone. Everyone can choose and walk this path, but very few actually have the strength, courage, discipline, and perseverance to do what it takes to walk it. That is what sets them apart. That is what makes them legends, heroes, champions, leaders, and saints.

—◈—

Rhythm or no rhythm, life isn't always easy. Sometimes I find myself deliriously happy. I have had many mountain top experiences, but life isn't always lived on the mountaintops of the world. Sometimes we find ourselves in the valleys of fear and doubt, or in the abyss of suffering and loneliness. At those times it is easy to become discouraged, to abandon *The Way*, to let the critics get you down. At those times, travel in your mind to a small orphanage in Calcutta, and on a wall there you will find these words:

People are unreasonable, illogical, and self-centered.
LOVE THEM ANYWAY
If you do good, people will accuse you of
selfish, ulterior motives.
DO GOOD ANYWAY
If you are successful, you win false friends
and true enemies.
SUCCEED ANYWAY
The good you do will be forgotten tomorrow.
DO GOOD ANYWAY
Honesty and frankness make you vulnerable.
BE HONEST AND FRANK ANYWAY
Big people with even bigger ideas will be shot down
by small people with even smaller minds.
THINK BIG ANYWAY
People favor underdogs, but follow only top dogs.

BE THE UNDERDOG ANYWAY
What you spent years building may be
destroyed overnight.
BUILD ANYWAY
People really need help
but may attack you if you help them.
HELP THEM ANYWAY
Give the world the best you have
and you'll get kicked in the teeth.
**GIVE THE WORLD THE BEST
YOU'VE GOT ANYWAY.**

LET YOUR LIGHT SHINE

In the process of writing this book I have returned to
Austria on a couple of occasions. I have returned to
Gaming and to the former monastery where I discovered
life anew. Now I have shared with you, as I promised
myself I would, what I discovered there in the mountains a couple of hours outside of Vienna—*The Rhythm
of Life.*

What is contained in these pages has the power to
change your life. I know, because these ideas have
changed my life, and continue to enrich my life
everyday.

I know a woman who has carried her passport around
with her for thirty-four years. She has never used it, but
she never goes anywhere without it tucked safely away
inside her handbag.

Thirty-four years ago she had an opportunity to take
a trip, but for many reasons at the last minute she decided
not to. She never will take that trip, and she will always
regret not having taken it when she had the chance.

You are holding a passport in your hands right now, with valid visas to higher levels of consciousness and more abundant living. I know it is a valid passport—I have used it myself. But, it is not enough just to have a passport. You must make the journey. Be confident. Do not be afraid. Have courage. Take it one step at a time. Make the journey.

A life well invested has few regrets. A life lived richly has few apologies to make. Find *The Rhythm of Life*.

—⁓—

If you have come this far, you have obviously found some value in the ideas that fill these pages. Don't set this book down now on a shelf to gather dust. Start again. Keep it near to you. When you come to the end for a second time, start again. Read five pages a day perpetually. Make it a lifelong companion. It is the only way for the ideas to take root in our practical everyday lives.

I have tried to fill these pages with ideas that we can read over and over again, each time revealing a new layer of meaning. They are ideas that resonate deeper within us each time we read them—and even deeper again, when we take the time to slowly and quietly reflect on them.

As the ideas in this book begin to change your life— as you begin to experience the power of *The Rhythm of Life*—share this book. Give a copy to a friend as a gift. Suggest it to your family. Help others discover *The Rhythm of Life*. Remember, there are two seas in Palestine...

—⁓—

Rarely does a day go by when I don't think of my high school motto—*Luceat Lux Vestra*. It is Latin, taken from the fifth chapter of Matthew's Gospel, and means "Let Your Light Shine."

The legends, heroes, leaders, champions, and saints that we have spoken of throughout this book, and who fill the pages of our history books, are just symbols of the goodness and greatness that is within us all.

Do not let your life be like a shooting star which lights up the sky for only a brief moment.

Let your life be like the sun that always burns brightly in the heavens, bringing light and warmth to all those on earth.

———

Let *your* light shine.

If you would like to order additional copies of this book, are interested in writing to the author, wish to receive his newsletter, would like information about his speaking engagements, or would like to invite him to speak to your group, please address all correspondence to:

THE MATTHEW KELLY FOUNDATION
1648 Ridge Avenue, Suite 2
Steubenville, Ohio 43952